ŀ
A Memoi ...ıu Jecrets

## "A beautiful memoir from the heart..."

Nancy Salz has written a beautiful memoir from the heart about her search to recover the nanny she loved like a mother, a woman who raised her and whose memory stayed with her long after the flesh and blood person had disappeared from her life. In an era in which many women rely on others to help raise their children—or work raising the children of others—this book provides a new and important perspective on this kind of relationship. We know that children bond to their caregivers. But Salz takes this universal truth and shows it in a new light, thanks to her particular and moving story of her relationship with Miss Hanna.

— Malena Watrous, author of *If You Follow Me*

## "Beautifully written, poignant"

Nancy Salz's beautifully written, poignant story reminds us convincingly of the vital importance of at least one consistently attentive loving adult in the life of every child. Since improving mothering customs in the United States has been my professional passion, I cannot recommend it strongly enough.

— Alice Kahn Ladas, Ed.D., psychologist focusing on early childhood trauma; co-author of *The G Spot: And Other Discoveries About Human Sexuality*

### *"Powerful ... wrenching"*

Nancy Salz's *Nanny. A Memoir of Love and Secrets* begins and ends with the author's relationship with Miss Hanna, a middle-aged lady who raised her from birth into adolescence, as a professional governess, but a loving one—the only source of human warmth in a singularly loveless household. This brief, but powerful book goes far beyond the Salz home and offers an extraordinarily vivid and detailed account of Manhattan in the 1940s and 50s from the point of view of the young daughter of wealthy residents of the Upper East Side. The young Ms. Salz's powers of observation—of sounds, smells, and minute visual details—are almost superhuman, and so are the mature Ms. Salz's memory and precision in translating them into prose. Anyone with a historical interest in the New York of these decades will find rich rewards here. And then there is the wrenching story of a prosperous, but deeply unhappy family and the woman who did her best over the years to care for its children.

#### — Michael Miller, Editor, *New York Arts/Berkshire Review*

### *"A book to be cherished"*

In this sensitively written memoir, Nancy Salz brings readers on an investigative journey into the tragic childhood of Salz's own late, beloved governess. Nanny is a wonderful debut: the story of the intense bond between a child and her governess, and an account of how one woman's attempt to understand the past leads her into a fuller understanding of herself. This is a book to be cherished.

#### — James Arthur, author of *Charms Against Lightning*

# ❖ NANNY ❖
## A Memoir of Love and Secrets

For Julie — my dear friend,
teacher and fellow student. I
wouldn't be a writer without you.
Thank
you

# ❖ NANNY ❖

## A Memoir of Love and Secrets

Love, Nancy

# N A N C Y   S A L Z

**RICHARD BOOKS**
New York City

Richard Books
New York City

ISBN 978-0-9960207-0-1
eBook ISBN 978-0-9960207-1-8

Photo of New York Cancer Hospital courtesy of Memorial Sloan Kettering Cancer Center. Used by Permission.

Photo of North Street, Middletown, from the book *Middletown* (Marvin H. Cohen, Arcadia Publishing, 2001). Courtesy of Marvin H. Cohen. Used by permission.

All other photos courtesy of the author.

Printed in the United States of America

www.richardbooks.com

246897531

First Edition

Book and cover design by Susan Newman Design, Inc.

For Miss Hanna
And
For Richard and Wendy

Where does a person live?

In our feelings?

In our image of her world?

In our memories?

In her own right?

# 1

The winter sun bore into my black coat, warmed through my sweater, my skin and into my spirit. It was the kind of sun that made me want to stop in my tracks, point my face upward through the New York City skyscrapers and just bask.

But my emotions were already a block and a half in front of me—skipping down the street like a five-year-old girl. This was the first day of my search for my former governess, my nanny, my human umbilical cord to the normal world, the woman whom I had loved more than I loved my own mother. She had saved my life. After decades I was determined to unearth every detail I could find about her. Although she had raised me since birth, I knew only three facts about her: she was Catholic; she had grown up in an orphanage; and she had died in St. Rose's Home, a lower-Manhattan cancer hospice.

I hurried past the wooden and wrought-iron benches in Thomas Paine Park across from the New York Supreme Court Building, the courthouse with the tall steps where many scenes from *Law & Order* are filmed, and headed toward the New York City Office of Vital Records on Worth Street, about a block away. My plan was to obtain a copy of my nanny's death certificate, which I assumed would contain the names of her parents. A good place to begin the search for her story, I thought.

On that sunny, spring-like morning in January, while stopped by a flashing red "don't walk" sign, I started to shiver. Real, teeth-chattering shakes that frightened and puzzled me. I stepped back to be near a concrete building I could hold on to and waited to feel better. As I stared down at the feet and shadows of the lawyers and potential jurors who rushed by, I tried to understand what was happening. I quickly ruled out illness; I didn't feel sick or even faint. I doubted

I was having a panic attack. I'd had a few of those decades earlier; the feelings weren't the same. Within a few seconds I recognized that my shivering had to be psychological: fear, most likely—but fear of what? The usual causes of my deepest fears, my parents and brother, had died years before. Whatever this shivering was, it had to be outdated and irrational. Slowly I started to laugh at myself. It seemed the search for my nanny was going to be an adventure into all kinds of unknown territory. I let go of the building and continued on my way. Although I now ignored them, the shivers persisted until I entered the Office of Vital Records.

Inside it was as stuffy, hot, and crowded as a bank at lunchtime. The chairs and desks were metal and old. The walls couldn't have been painted since Fiorello LaGuardia was mayor. After waiting in a long, serpentine line to pay a fee, I was steered to another room where I approached the desk of the person in charge, a plump, gray-haired woman, tidy and efficient, clad appropriately in a white blouse and black skirt. She asked me the approximate date of my nanny's death, then stood up, reached to a shelf behind her and handed me a four-inch-thick, black book of all the people who had died around that year.

After nearly dropping the heavy volume onto the hanging wall shelf that was designated for visitors, I pulled up a chair and searched its pages—first by year, then by month. Each page had three columns of close to a hundred names each in tiny type. Finally under October, midway down the first column of a page, I found her:

Elizabeth Hanna. Died October 7, 1957.

The moment I saw her name I broke down in quiet, gentle sobs. This was the first time in decades that I felt I was in my nanny's presence. She had actually lived and died. In a bare, bureaucratic room, I reconnected with that part of myself that I most cherished. I felt solid, real, and confident. As I reached for a Kleenex in my bag, all I wanted was to be held by my warm, safe memories.

## 2.

Her full name was Elizabeth Cecilia Hanna; we called her Miss Hanna. One spring day in 1940 she arrived on the stoop of my family's Upper East Side limestone town house near Park Avenue. She had all her belongings in one suitcase, or two at the most. She was a small, forty-five-year-old woman with olive skin, a long nose, and a short forehead. Her hair was mostly gray and had unruly strands that sprang from the buns she twisted and pinned to her head, one above each ear.

I can imagine her standing on the purple cement stoop, her deep-set, dark eyes reflecting her past but revealing none of its details. She appears neither happy nor unhappy, neither excited nor apprehensive as she waits for the door to open. Inside the house are new parents to answer to, new children to take care of, a new place to live—for a while. She is accepting. This is her work. She has been a nanny for many years.


Miss Hanna had been hired by my parents to take care of my nearly three-year-old brother and me, about to be born. Her only private space in this sixteen-foot-wide, five-story residence was to be a tiny room on the fourth floor separated by French doors from a much grander room, which would be mine.

At that time, upper-middle-class parents desiring caregivers for their children didn't usually choose "nannies" like those in *The Nanny Diaries*, temporary young women who stayed just a few years. They hired "governesses" or "nurses," older life-long professionals who took care of their charges—frequently loving them as their own—until they were no longer needed. Then they moved on to another family. All my parents' friends employed nannies, and all my childhood friends had one.

My mother Elisabeth, called Betty, and my father Jacque had been married for seven years when Miss Hanna arrived, but were still only 25 and 28 years old. They were proud of belonging to a social set of other well-off, second-generation Jewish young-married couples who lived on the Upper East Side of Manhattan and summered on the Jersey shore. Their lifestyle of beautiful homes, catered parties, stylish clothes, multiple servants, fancy cars—and among the women, gossip, always gossip—defined the culture of our home. Like a teenager in high school, my beautiful mother imitated the behavior of her peers. Their mores determined how she judged, pushed, and punished her own children. Miss Hanna was not of that world, but it was the world of my family that she walked into.

My father was five feet six with a round body and face—a face that grew so much rounder with each passing year that when he took his glasses off they left ridges in the skin next to his eyes. He resembled his shorter father, James, who had Americanized his name from Jacob soon after he arrived in this country. Jacque both loved and resented his father.

"My father made me work for a whole year to save money for a bicycle," he told us around the dinner table. He repeated this story every few months. "But when I'd saved enough for the bicycle, he wouldn't let me buy it. He made me put the money in a savings account instead."

When he was making his own money, my father bought a Rolls-Royce as a substitute for the bicycle his bullying father had denied him.

James had immigrated to America in 1903, following by a year his younger brother, Ignatz. They came from Tarnow, in the Austrian occupied section of Poland. Together they started a successful business, Salz Brothers Pens, which later became the Stratford Pen Company. James met my grandmother, Laura, a buxom, pretty lady with fine manners, when he was on a sales trip to San Francisco. Laura was born there in 1883, as was her mother twenty years earlier. James and Laura married in 1910 and made their first home in New

York City near the Hudson River on West 111th Street.

In 1928, when my father was seventeen, James, né Jacob, died of a heart attack. As was the custom of the time, Laura soon married her husband's brother Ignatz, who was gentle and soft-spoken with a lilting German accent. He had loved Laura from afar for years. Ignatz was the grandfather I knew.

It's hard to believe that this sweet man, who sipped coffee through a piece of hard sugar held in his teeth, had in his days as a nightclub-frequenting bachelor in New York City been nearly killed by hit men hired by the husband of a woman with whom he had been having an affair. The story was covered for four consecutive days by the *New York Times*.

On the evening of January 14, 1927, Iggy, as he was called, heard a knock on his apartment door and opened it to two men who immediately shot him in the stomach. James, his brother, insisted that the motive was robbery, although neither $4,000 in cash in the apartment nor Iggy's diamond ring and stickpin were missing. James also tried to convince the police that Iggy had been mistaken for a

Federal narcotics squad agent living in the same building on West 77th Street.

Three days after the shooting James offered a $5,000 reward for the capture of the gunmen. He also told the *New York Times* that he would hire private detectives to find the hit men, but he never did. The police established that the motive was revenge for Iggy's affair. The perpetrators were never caught.

Iggy survived peritonitis from the shot to his abdomen, but during a summer European vacation when he was seventy-eight he developed an abscess at the site of the gunshot wound. He returned to his and Laura's home in Deal on the Jersey shore, leaving Laura in Europe attended by her other son, my uncle Irwin. The abscess led to Iggy's death a few days after he returned. I was eighteen years old and was invited into his room the day before he died. He was white as the bedsheets beneath his chin, but at the time I didn't realize that meant he was close to death.

A dark wood Rococo desk where he wrote checks in slanted, German handwriting remained in the room next to mine in New Jersey to remind me of my grandfather, who was plump and adorable all the time I knew him.

A few days after Iggy's death, as I was preparing to go down the stairs in New Jersey, I was stopped by the sounds of my father crying in the living room. My father never cried—as far as I knew—and I was riveted to my place at the top of the stairs too frightened to move until he stopped. I wonder now, had I gone down the stairs and put my arms around him, if he would have let me comfort him. More likely he would have hidden his feelings and resumed his posture as the invulnerable ruler of the family. My parents never revealed their vulnerability to their children. Decades later, in the days after my father died, my mother dried her tears whenever she saw me approach.

I was a proud sophomore at Vassar College two years after Iggy's death when my father drove up for Fathers' Weekend. I loved showing him the ivy-covered dorms as we walked around the campus and having dinner with my roommate and her father. We were never that close before or after. My father had encouraged me to study hard during high school, especially since my brother was such a terrible student. I remember asking him to read my essay for high school English class. He sent me back to my room to rewrite it, saying I could do better and then praising me when I did. He encouraged me on several occasions and motivated me to get good grades and aim high in my choice of college. When I showed him my best report card, he said,

"If only you were my son."

He said that often, oblivious to how that comment made me feel as a girl, as the less-valued child. I know he was proud of me even if being a daughter was second best. "Any cat can have kittens" was one of his favorite maxims. To me that meant all women were interchangeable and were valued only for procreation abilities.

My father enjoyed his mean streak. It made him feel important, a feeling he did not have among his friends, most of whom had more money than he did. Once he threw Jimmy's and my allowance on the floor to show his power over us. He smirked as we crawled on the green carpet at his feet to pick it up. And he thought it was funny when the tenants in the loft building he owned repeatedly got stuck in the barely standard elevators he installed. When I challenged his meanness, he cut me off:

"Don't disrespect your father," he said.

"Stop talking, Nancy," my mother pleaded. "Do it for me."

I did stop talking—for her. It was too late to stop disrespecting my father. He was able to terrify me, but he never inspired respect.

At the dinner table my father talked in unpunctuated, uninterruptable sentences, going on about the people he knew; about their money, which he admired and envied; about himself. Some of these people found him fascinating as a raconteur, but I hated my role as his audience. I wanted to talk about myself and whatever interested me at the moment. If I said, "I learned today that there's lots of oil in Texas," he would have replied, "Joey Pearberg is in the oil business. I know Joey very well. Joey is a dear friend of mine. Only last week ...," and he would be off and running.

I challenged my father to be the center of attention and won just often enough to keep me trying. I knew well enough to talk about subjects he liked, mostly money and business.

I asked him about his investing adviser, who had published several books and whose intellect I admired from afar.

My brother Jimmy rarely got a word in edgewise. He said very little at the dinner table, constantly on guard against my father. It was painful to watch him shrivel under my father's disapproval. As the oldest—and as the son—he was showered with gifts, money, attention, and special privileges, like once taking a girl on a date in the Rolls-Royce, which he crashed after dropping her home. (I cringed for him.) My father also prodded and criticized him in the hope of making him a success. But not too much of a success. My father yearned for him to be a winner but was threatened if Jimmy even came close to overshadowing him. As a girl, my successes, my good grades, were merely girl-successes, no threat at all, to his thinking. By the time Jimmy was sixteen he had flunked out of two high schools and had started drinking socially. In his early twenties he became a full-fledged alcoholic unable to hold down a job. My father had to support him and resented Jimmy every month when he handed him a check, as he did for the rest of Jimmy's life.

Somewhere, somehow Jimmy found an inner strength. It couldn't help him make a living, but it enabled him to achieve and maintain sobriety beginning in his early forties—far harder than mere work. He was sober for fourteen years before he died of stomach cancer, perhaps related to his drinking. He refused pain pills nearly until his death because he didn't want to become addicted to them. He lived only until his fifty-fifth year.

As much as my mother tried to teach me my place as a girl and future woman, I refused to stay in it. As a child, especially a girl-child, I might have been better off had I been less confrontational, less competitive with my father— more subservient, more submissive, more lady-like, like my mother. On the outside, I learned to be quiet, to submit to their control. On the inside my anger festered. When I returned to my room after an argument with my parents, Miss Hanna often saw my reactions, but she never talked against my parents. I didn't need her to say anything. Just being with her comforted me.

## 3

As a child I often gazed up at my mother, Betty, from the gray marble step that led up to her en-suite bathroom, which was covered in deep-rose-colored tile and trimmed in black tile along the top. Even the sink and tub were deep rose. The centerpiece of this bathroom was her dressing table, covered in mirrors on all surfaces including drawer facings and leg panels. A triptych of mirrors, angled so that my mother could see herself from three directions, sat on the table. Every time she sat down on the matching stool—also covered with mirrors on the seat and on the sides of legs— she was surrounded by her beauty, reflected back to her again and again.

Her dressing table was custom-made for her, an elegant woman in the Princess Grace style—her sleek hair pulled back to show off her big, blue eyes. She had been a model in her late teens for one of the most prestigious modeling agencies of the time, John Robert Powers. From my seat on the step I stared up in awe as she carefully put on her makeup: the powder, the rouge, the eyebrow pencil, the cake mascara she sometimes spit into to make it wet and ready to apply—and, of course, her lipstick: how carefully she placed it on the bow of her lip and dabbed and dabbed it until her lips were covered.

Finally, her beauty enhanced by makeup, my mother walked to the mirror over the sink to attend to her long hair. By the time I was seven her dark hair had become blond, and I had forgotten that it was ever otherwise. She carefully teased most of her hair into the style of the day, then combed the remaining strands over the tease and pulled it through a mesh doughnut at the nape of her neck. Using fingers and hairpins she tucked here and pulled there to make a perfect chignon. Holding her small hand mirror, encircled by its smoky white plastic handle, she turned around and made sure every hair was perfectly in place, lightly placing the comb on top of rather than through her hair. Later, when hair spray was invented, she sprayed her hair all over so that no errant breeze could disturb the perfection.

I was so intimidated by her beauty and glamour that by the time I was eight I had given up any hope that I could grow up to be like her. It was too big a reach. She was blond. I had dark hair. People told me I was pretty, but I didn't believe them. Everyone knew it was better to be blond. She competed with her friends and won not only at tennis and golf but also at beauty and style. Only when I was thirty-two and a friend asked me if my mother was a natural blond did I remember her touching up her roots with peroxide and her weekly trips to the Breck salon on 57th Street.

I determined early on that I would try to be a good student instead of beautiful, and be like my father instead of my mother. This was my fallback position, not my first choice—but one position at which I thought I could succeed even if it wasn't how girls were supposed to be in the 1950s. As a fifth-grader I saw an ad in the *New York Times* for a free booklet about Alaska. The booklet would be helpful for a school report I was writing. But I thought no company would send an informational item to a girl. Girls were meant to be pretty, not scholarly. So I sent away for the booklet and used the name Johnny Salz on the return address. In my report card I was commended for my independent research.

My mother was the oldest daughter, the middle child, of Theodor Blum, an oral surgeon, and Bertha ("Birdie") Blum of West 79th Street in New York City. Theodor had emigrated from Vienna, Birdie from Budapest. They met and married here. Their plans for their oldest child, Oscar, were that he would become an oral surgeon like his father, who had helped introduce the use of novocaine in America. Oscar disappointed them when he ended up in the pen business with my father. Their youngest child, Ruth-Elaine, would be "the smart one"; she fulfilled her destiny by graduating from Barnard. Betty, my mother, was anointed "the pretty one" and was groomed to marry a rich man. She was taught to be beautiful and submissive. Although she was smart—she graduated from the Fieldston School and read one or two books a month, mostly best-selling novels like *Forever*

*Amber,* in addition to the *New Yorker*—only her social skills and looks were valued by her mother. Her feelings and self-awareness, what we now call "emotional intelligence," were left as dormant as an unwatered seed. Yet my mother thrived before she was married. She was fun and popular, captain of the tennis team at Fieldston. She told me that her high school days were the happiest of her life.

Theodor made a comfortable living but lost most of his money in the 1929 stock market crash. This may have been a cause of my grandparents' divorce. Family lore has it that after Theodor walked my mother down the aisle in 1934 he kept right on walking. For years my mother wouldn't speak to him. She became very close to her mother, a woman who smoked all the time and had a phlegm-y, hacking cough that in later years became my impetus to stop smoking.

My father's ego ballooned when he married a beautiful woman, and my mother's ballooned when she snagged a rich husband. They may have been in love. Photos show them happy on their honeymoon. Mother told me how much fun they had in their first apartment at 929 Park Avenue eating apples in bed and throwing the cores out their open bedroom window.

But soon "the pretty one" discovered that her beauty gave her no power at home. It could not help her care for a difficult husband and run a household. She was frequently overwhelmed. It turned out that the beautiful, outgoing, popular girl had married a man who disliked going out with other couples. He just wanted to stay home. When my mother wanted them to join a golf club in New Jersey, where we lived with my father's mother and uncle Iggy during the summer, my father was too frightened to go to the club to meet the friends who would propose them for membership. They met instead on my father's fifteen-foot yacht, which he owned for just a few years. He went into therapy for a while, and, afterwards was happier among people. But at home he demanded all of my mother's attention. I used to watch her turn her face away from him and purse her lips to hide her anger. She tried to hide her feelings but I knew she was angry much of the time. For a few years, before I was ten, she screamed at us at the slightest provocation. I wonder if she suspected that my father had been having affairs since their engagement. (My father confided them to my brother when

Jimmy was 23, and I learned of them when I was in my late thirties after my father bragged about them to me.)

My brother Jimmy was born three years into the marriage. A few days after his birth he developed diarrhea, a serious illness in a baby. He stayed in the hospital for weeks, and once he came home, he never stopped crying. Following her pediatrician's trendy advice, my mother would leave Jimmy crying in his crib so as not to spoil him. It went against all of her motherly instincts, but she did what she was told. Even years later she bemoaned, "I never picked him up; that poor little boy."

She never had to worry about picking me up. Miss Hanna took care of that.

# 4

Before I was five and started school, Miss Hanna and I were always together. Just the two of us. America entered World War II in 1941 when I was a year-and-a-half old, and my mother was away a few days a week working as a volunteer driver in the WAVES, Women Accepted for Volunteer Emergency Service. She donned her blue-gray uniform and drove Captain Gene Tunney, the former boxer, who was stationed in the Throgs Neck section of the Bronx, wherever he needed to go. She thrived on all the flirtations sent her way. The gas rationing stamps that came with the job allowed our family to drive to New Jersey in the summer.

My father's factory switched from making fountain pens to making parts for war equipment. His company was considered vital to the war effort, and he was excused from active service. His brother, Irwin, served in the signal corps in England training carrier pigeons. For years after he returned home, he kept pigeon coops in our New Jersey gardens.

My mother's brother Oscar was a naval officer in Europe; he married an English woman he met during the war. My mother's brother-in-law, Sam, was an Army officer serving in the Pacific.

We had blackouts on the Jersey shore where we spent the summers with my grandparents. The near-weekly air raid sirens that sounded soon after the sun went down were terrifying. The wailing, the loudness drove me into my bed and under my covers, where I could still hear everything. Miss Hanna pulled down the shades in my room—a formidable task. Instead of windows my second-floor room had ten sets of thin doors opening onto two narrow balconies; twenty shades in all. I lay in bed hoping that each scream of the sirens would be the last. Miss Hanna told me that Germans might be off the coast in boats, and we learned years later that they were. Miss Hanna may have been as frightened as I, but she told me there was nothing to fear. Only when the sirens stopped was I able to fall asleep.

In New York City, Miss Hanna spoke a lot about an American Nazi organization founded in 1936 called the German-American Bund. A branch was located in Yorkville, just a few blocks away from where we lived. She hated them—and all Germans, including my friends' governesses who had emigrated from Germany. She remembered the Bund marching down 86th Street in the late 1930s, just four blocks north of our home.

We were aware of the war but were mostly unaffected by it. Until I was six Miss Hanna and I ate dinner with our cook Joe in the kitchen on the first floor while my parents and brother ate in the dining room on the second floor. I told her about school, about my friends, everything that happened to me during my day. On Joe's nights off, usually Thursdays and Sundays, my parents and Jimmy went off to the Longchamps restaurant on Madison Avenue between 78th and 79th Streets for dinner. When the front door closed, I was left behind with Miss Hanna alone in that big house. She made us sandwiches, or we ate a dinner that Joe had left for us. My parents explained that I couldn't go out to dinner because I was too young. It all seemed so unfair. I felt left out and unworthy. My psychological separation from my family began with those nights—as did my feelings of loyalty to Miss Hanna.

*If I am not a part of your family,* I thought, *then I will be a family with Miss Hanna and Joe. My parents belong to Jimmy, but Miss Hanna belongs to me. She is mine.*

Reinforced over the years, even when I was six and allowed to join my parents and brother in the dining room, my feelings of alienation from my family and my loyalty to Miss Hanna grew in tandem. The closer I grew to Miss Hanna the more it irritated my mother:

"How can you love that ugly woman?" she often asked me.

"Miss Hanna holds my head when I vomit and you don't," I once yelled.

"Well go upstairs and vomit now so I can hold your head," she said.

I ran upstairs to cry to Miss Hanna, but she stopped me. Not only would she never say anything against my parents to me, but she would never allow me to criticize my parents to her.

Eventually I couldn't even talk about Miss Hanna to my mother. I only had to start a sentence with "Miss Hanna says …" to hear my mother say,

"Why do you care what that stupid woman thinks?"

Sometimes I talked about Miss Hanna just to tweak my mother's jealousy, as I came to understand when I was older. But the feelings engendered by my mother's cruel comments made the exercise too painful—my little jabs weren't worth it.

My mother thought she could shame my love for Miss Hanna out of me. She couldn't. Instead my love dove for cover deep inside me like a naughty puppy slinking off to hide under the sofa. As her ridicule persisted, the love went deeper.

To protect it, I made a steadfast promise to myself at age seven: I would never talk about Miss Hanna to anyone, especially my mother. I would never let my mother or any of my friends know how much I loved Miss Hanna. Sometimes early on when provoked by my mother, I would slip and break my promise. "Don't you say that about her," I would scream in response to my mother's venom.

As I got older, it became easier to keep my feelings about Miss Hanna to myself. Little by little, shored up by my innate obstinacy and my refusal to betray my attachment to Miss Hanna, the promise grew stronger until it became an indestructible vow. The vow became my secret and it kept my mouth shut and my feelings about Miss Hanna hidden from everyone for over fifty years.

And so it came to be from the earliest days I can remember, Miss Hanna's role was to take care of me as best she could—keep me fed, dressed, clean and loved—and my role was to protect her as best I could by keeping our deep bond a secret.

I sensed Miss Hanna was providing me with the essentials of warmth and decency I would need in the real world outside my family, outside their social circle. She wasn't like my family. She was more like the teachers at school and my school friends' parents: concerned about people, feelings, and character—talking less about clothes, dinner parties, clubs, who was socially acceptable and who was not.

My parents' friends sent their children to socially appropriate schools like Dalton and Brearley. Because my mother's father had been friends with one of the founders of the progressive and liberal Ethical Culture Fieldston School, and my mother had attended, my brother and I were sent there. Even in the lowest grades of grammar school we had ethics classes, discussing right and wrong, equality, justice, and fairness.

Early on I noticed the difference between our life, with its excesses and social whirlwind, and the lives of my fellow students. Our home was fashionable and decorated; my classmates' homes were book-filled and fitted out with older but more inviting furniture. I became increasingly aware of the contrast between my parents' and my lifestyle and the meager existences of Miss Hanna and Joe. It was unfair. Clearly the ethical culture of the school took root in me much more than it had in my mother.

In winter, Miss Hanna and I spent most sunny days in Central Park. She found a protected spot behind the Metropolitan Museum of Art near 79th Street. There, then, in wartime 1940s, sheltered from the wind and with warmth radiating from the white stone sides of the museum, my park friends and I could play hopscotch, jump rope, and take off our coats in the middle of winter.

Sometimes we went to a playground on 84th Street that was equipped with swings, slides, and a wooden seesaw that gave mean, deep splinters. For a special treat we walked down to the Mary Harriman Rumsey Playground, near the East Drive and 72nd Street in Central Park. This playground had all the usual attractions plus a large sandbox, maybe twenty feet in diameter, surrounded by a wrought iron fence. It, too, had swings and seesaws—less splintery—and its paving was prettier, a white concrete riddled with light beige and deep tan stones instead of the smooth blacktop at the 84th Street playground.

Many days a friendly, mustached photographer roamed the park with a large, square camera atop a tripod resting on his shoulder. He asked Miss Hanna and the other governesses and mothers if he could take pictures of their charges. If the proofs turned out well, he sold the photos to the children's parents. He must have made appointments for the photos, or how could I have such a lovely photo of myself in my good lavender hat and coat—hardly playground attire?

I often accompanied Miss Hanna on her errands in the neighborhood surrounding our town house. On our way to the A&P on Madison Avenue, we passed the Burlington Bookstore. Its windows were packed solid—books were laid down along the bottom of each window and stacked on top of each other along the sides. Not being able to read never kept me from stopping and studying the colorful covers. A few windows south was Campbell's funeral home with its deep maroon canopy and liveried doorman. Across from Campbell's we dropped off ailing shoes at the cobbler's between 80th and 81st Streets; that store smelled of leather and pungent glue.

The very next door was the A&P. It wasn't a supermarket as we'd think of one today. The floor was covered with sawdust, and cans and boxes were arranged on shelves as high as the ceiling. We had to ask a clerk for each item we wanted. He roamed the store, grabbed each of our requests from its shelf, and set it on a wooden counter, where we waited so we could tell him what to get for us next. Sometimes he climbed a ladder. Other times he retrieved cans and packages with a long wooden pole topped with a pair of shiny metal grips that he controlled with a squeezable handle.

If my feet were starting to feel tight in my current shoes, we walked further down Madison to Indian Walk for new, larger shoes. I had a childhood crush on my salesman, Mr. Paine, who was movie-star-handsome in my eyes. Indian Walk also had a machine that X-rayed each child's foot to help the salesman find the perfect shoe, the perfect fit. For school days, Mr. Paine sold Miss Hanna and me my brown, lace-up shoes; for parties, black patent leather Mary Janes; and for summer, my favorite red sandals with tiny holes in a pattern on the top and straps that buckled at the sides. Years later he also sold me my first pair of heels.

When Miss Hanna needed shoes for herself, or clothes or underwear, we went to Third Avenue under the elevated train, the El. It was dark, smelly, and eerie—and just two blocks from the luxury of Park Avenue, sunny, attended by doormen, clean. I didn't mind going there, but I didn't like it either. I knew it was a poorer, working class neighborhood, and I felt uncomfortable. I didn't belong.

It wasn't just the noise, when trains on the El squealed on the tracks and clanked by, car by car, but also the soot that rained down on us into our hair and eyes. We frequently had to go to a nearby pharmacy to have the pharmacist remove a painful piece of dirt. New York City was much dirtier in those days. I got soot in my eye on Third and on Park Avenue too. But on Third Avenue the streets smelled sour like the trains. The black shadows of the El that were cast onto the buildings by the morning or afternoon light became covered by the moving shadows of the trains. Shadows moved over shadows. You could never see more than a few inches of daylight.

On Third Avenue Miss Hanna bought her Red

Cross brand shoes that laced up the front of her feet and had clunky heels about one inch high. She had white shoes that matched the white uniforms she wore for many years and black shoes for her own days-off outfits. Keeping her white shoes clean was an unending task. She polished and powdered them only to have to repeat the process in a few days. Years later she had special shoes made for her that wouldn't hurt her bunions. Miss Hanna had trouble with her feet and walked with her toes pointed out—an unforgivable sin in my mother's eyes.

"Walk with your feet pointing straight ahead. Don't walk the way Miss Hanna walks," my mother instructed.

I looked down at Miss Hanna's feet and my own feet and made sure to point my toes in the right direction to please my mother. It made me feel sad that Miss Hanna didn't walk the right way. I hoped no one else noticed or cared about her feet.

In the under-the-El underwear store, with shelves piled high with labeled containers, Miss Hanna's cotton underpants were boxed with other underpants of the same size. Miss Hanna always picked the same underpants: white cotton that came up to her waist. She also owned a pair of pink woolen pants that came down to her knees. She wore those over her white underpants on cold days along with her black, sleeveless, lightly quilted vest, which she called a "hug-me-tight," under her coat. The underwear store smelled musty. I felt bad that Miss Hanna had to shop there.

I knew I didn't belong in this neighborhood of what I thought were poor people but who were more likely middle-class, blue-collar workers. I had caught the snobbishness of my parents, and no amount of love for Miss Hanna could erase the feeling or the guilt it engendered. Even at four or five years of age, I preferred the style and color of Madison Avenue.

One day when I was four Miss Hanna took me to watch the St. Patrick's Day parade in front of the Metropolitan Museum on Fifth Avenue, down the street from our 1899 home with its bay window sticking out from the second floor living room. I must have let go of Miss Hanna's hand and pushed my way to the front of the crowd to better see the marchers and brass bands. Suddenly I couldn't find Miss Hanna. For a few seconds I was terrified until I saw a policeman. I was told that I could trust policemen.

"I'm lost," I cried to him. Then through my sobs added with pride, "I know where I live."

He lifted me up onto his shoulders and asked if I could see Miss Hanna. When I couldn't, he put me down and started to walk me home. But there was Miss Hanna on the street walking toward me—she looked frantic. She didn't punish me, but she gave me a good "talking to." I have loved policemen ever since.

It was many years before I again tried to leave Miss Hanna's side on the street, yet an urge to be independent grew stronger. Finally I begged Miss Hanna to let me walk on the street by myself—at least to mail a letter in the post office box hanging on a light pole on the corner. It was just half a block away, on my side of Madison Avenue across from the Burlington Bookstore. I wouldn't have to cross any streets. When I was seven she said yes, and on a sunny day I took off on my mini adventure past the other town houses and a Catholic convent that filled the block between 81st and 82nd on Madison.

On the way back from standing on tiptoe and carefully placing the letter in the box, a man stopped me in the street. He had light brown hair and was probably in his twenties.

"Little girl, will you put your hand into my pants through the zipper?" he said. "I'll give you a nickel."

I remember seeing white, and looking down at the sidewalk as I considered his offer for a second. I was more perplexed than frightened. No one had ever told me not to put my hand in a man's pants, but it didn't seem right.

"No," I said, and ran home.

Miss Hanna was at the door to greet me, and I told her what happened. I wonder now why she wasn't looking out for me from the stoop of our house. Perhaps she didn't want me to see her watching me. When I asked her what the man wanted, she told me that he wanted to urinate on my hand. But at the same time, she told me that if a man ever bothered me again I should kick him in the testicles. Soon thereafter she taught me the words "sex maniac" and for years I stared at men on the street to see if they were sex maniacs.

In winter, when it was more difficult to play outdoors with other children, Miss Hanna took me to visit the children of my parents' friends, most of whom lived in big apartments on Park Avenue. She stayed and talked to the other governesses, even the German ones, while we either played with our dolls or played Parcheesi, Monopoly, or games we made up. If I visited or attended parties with my school friends, who mostly lived on the West Side and didn't have nannies, Miss Hanna dropped me off and picked me up later. When everyone else got up and ran to their mothers who were picking them up, I got jealous. The few times my friends did see my mother, such as at a school parents' day, which she occasionally visited for a few hours, they told me how pretty she was. My pride in her beauty was always tempered by my jealousy of their having a mother who showed up for them. Beauty versus showing up. For me there was no contest.

Our summer home was in Deal, on the Jersey shore a few miles north of Asbury Park. Before I was five, I went to the public beach with Miss Hanna while my mother and Jimmy swam at the beach club. I think now that the reason I wasn't asked to accompany them was that I had a large birthmark on my leg. It covered most of the front of my thigh. Mother didn't have the courage to cope with it. She didn't want anyone to see even a tiny pimple on her face, and in later years, when she had small skin cancers removed, she stayed home until the wounds healed. It was difficult for her to have, no less be seen with, a less-than-perfect daughter.

I preferred going to the public beach anyway. I felt uncomfortable with my beautiful mother at her beach club. She waved to her friends as we headed to her cabana near the big pool, and I trailed along next to her, feeling out of place. She wanted me to keep up, but I didn't belong in her world, either.

Mother hadn't a clue how to take care of me. She couldn't braid my hair. She couldn't cook. She bought my clothes, but I pushed her hands away when she tried to button or zip me into them. She may have been good at tying the bows on my dresses, but I fidgeted and told her to hurry up. I didn't want her to touch me—or try to take Miss

Hanna's place.

She didn't love me the way Miss Hanna did—if she loved me at all. Somewhere inside I craved for her to love me like Miss Hanna did—to listen to me, to respect me, to show that I was significant to her—and got mad at her when she didn't. It never occurred to me that maybe she couldn't.

When I asked her for help dealing with a bullying clique of girls in grammar school who called themselves "The Greats," she told me to tell them, "I'm the Pullman and you're the freight."

I blamed my birthmark for my mother's distance and begged my parents to get rid of it. They took me to see many doctors but the birthmark couldn't be removed; it involved too many layers of skin. Miss Hanna came to my rescue with Lydia O'Leary Covermark, a waterproof makeup that allowed me to swim without worry and feel normal at the beach.

In summer a special treat was playing games on the boardwalk in Asbury Park after we rode on the Casino carousel and in the bumper boats. When I was five my friend Kay beat me at Skee-Ball. I was a sore loser. Miss Hanna took me aside and explained, "You shouldn't just be unhappy that you lost but also be happy for your friend who won." Hours later when I found that happiness inside me, I proudly told her, "I'm glad Kay won." This was the first time of many that Miss Hanna taught me about giving and love.

Miss Hanna called the hottest summer nights "scorchers." Although Jimmy's room and my parents' room had air conditioning, mine did not. No air conditioner would fit in the narrow door-windows. Miss Hanna made me feel cooler by rubbing my arms, legs, body, and neck with alcohol that cooled my skin as it evaporated. Later in the evening, when a breeze blew in off the ocean two blocks away, she covered me with a sheet while I was sleeping.

One afternoon when I was seven, in the early evening of a summer day in New Jersey, I got a pain in my side that no amount of throwing up or bouts of diarrhea would relieve. Miss Hanna alerted my mother, who called our doctor. He rushed over to the house and into my room where I was lying on my bed. He pushed his hand into the right side of my abdomen, and my leg shot up and nearly kicked him in the head. I was having an appendicitis attack. My mother ran from my bedside to call her father, an oral surgeon, for the name of a good surgeon at nearby Long Branch Memorial Hospital. There was some talk of an ambulance, but Mother and Father drove me to the hospital themselves. If no cars were coming, they didn't stop for the red lights. I was frightened but excited about all the attention from my parents. After an emergency appendectomy, I woke up in the recovery room with Miss Hanna sitting patiently and watching over me. My parents had gone home.

The doctors said I was one of the first civilians to receive penicillin. It was a thick, white liquid painfully injected into my buttocks twice a day when I was in the hospital. I came home after a week, and the first moment I was left alone and unobserved I did a cartwheel, one of my favorite moves. I shudder now to think what I could have done to myself. Even Miss Hanna got mad at me.


Although my brother Jimmy, a handsome little boy with dark hair like mine, sometimes visited the Bronx Zoo with Miss Hanna and me, his goal in life was to distance himself as frequently as possible from his baby sister to show he was too old for a nanny. One day when I was eight or so he barged into my room.

"They're going to fire her," he taunted.

*What does that mean?* I wondered. It couldn't be good; Jimmy sounded so superior. Dumbstruck, I stared down at my gray flowered rug, past Jimmy to my pine toy box, at my gray chair, at my antique cherry spindle bed. Were they going to set Miss Hanna on fire? That was scary enough until I grasped the real concept. They could make Miss Hanna go away. I had never imagined—and could never imagine—my life without Miss Hanna. Starting that day I began to fear that if I was bad or got angry—or, worse yet, if I defended Miss Hanna—she would be fired. I would be alone. The fear grew. I threw up more often—every few weeks—and hunkered down into my vow of silence. My life, my safety changed forever. I hadn't lost her—she wasn't fired—but now I knew I could. She may have been mine, but I was not hers. I belonged to my parents, to *their* family.

Miss Hanna was not part of that family. That's something I always knew in theory, but I had never thought

◆

of her as a servant before, a servant who could be fired. I saw Miss Hanna and my mother together only rarely. Once they were having a conversation in my room in New York. My mother was just five feet three but she seemed to tower over Miss Hanna. She was the boss speaking to her uniformed servant.

We had two servants, a maid and a cook; three, if you count Miss Hanna. Joe, our cook, whom I adored, loved to make my favorite foods for me. He got up extra early to make my breakfast before school. Joe was a short black man who loved to laugh and giggle. When he got older and lost his front teeth, he wouldn't smile without his hand over his mouth. He had been a cook in the same unit in which my father's brother, Irwin, served during World War II. Irwin hired him after the war. Because Irwin was gay and felt he couldn't live openly in America, he moved to Europe in the early 1950s. Joe then came to us. Irwin returned to America about ten years later with Burk Wagner, a man he would live with until Burk died of AIDS, but Joe stayed in our home. He retired when my parents moved to Florida. They continued to pay him. Joe had been with my family for nearly thirty years.

Joe died when I was in my mid-forties. Irwin and I took the Metroliner to Philadelphia to attend his funeral. I loved that we went together. We were the only white people at the funeral. Joe's casket was open; when it was my turn I gathered my courage and stepped to the front of the chapel. Wanting to say good-bye to him overcame my squeamishness at looking at a dead person. He still looked like Joe—maybe a little fatter and older. I think I loved him, too. Irwin had been appointed a pallbearer by Joe's sister, and he accepted his assignment with grace. With Joe's casket on their shoulders, Irwin and the other pallbearers slowly walked on the dusty ground toward his grave. It was a pathetic cemetery, treeless, with only a few patches of grass sprouting up here and there. Joe deserved better.

Joe lived with us in the house on 82nd Street. His bedroom was on the fifth floor, the floor above Jimmy, Miss Hanna, and me. The fifth floor was only a half floor, really, with two tiny bedrooms and a small bathroom. It faced out on the roof over my room, Miss Hanna's room, the stairwell, the bathroom, and the linen closet. Two skylights, covered with chicken wire, provided a dull, gray light for the stairwell and the closet and part of the bathroom.

We had several maids in succession who each came and left after a few years. They cleaned house and served us dinner but didn't live in. By the time my father's business went into decline and was sold in the early 1950s, we had just a cleaning woman who came in a few days a week. Joe sent dinner up to the dining room for us in serving dishes on the pantry dumbwaiter. (By the age of six I was allowed to eat with my parents.) Dinners weren't fancy: chicken or meat, potatoes, vegetables, salad, and usually fruit for dessert. Mother and I took the serving dishes off and put them on the dinner table. After dinner, my father and Jimmy loaded a dishwasher in the pantry next to the dining room.

Living in a town house created separate spaces and separate lives. Vertical living, it's called. Children on the top floor. Parents and the den on the third floor. Dining and living rooms on the second floor. Foyer, kitchen, and laundry room on the first floor. If we had all been on the same floor, I wonder if we would have been a closer family. We certainly would have gotten in each other's lives more often—and in each other's way.

Miss Hanna stayed with Jimmy and me on the fourth floor and in the kitchen. My mother generally came upstairs only once a week, to get bedsheets and towels from the linen closet; my father climbed the flight of stairs to see us at most once a year. Jimmy and I played with our toys in our own rooms, not in the living room, which was used only when company came.

The dining room, with its large black and white tiled floor, its midnight-blue walls, and its towering breakfront filled with a full set of black, gold, and orange Royal Crown Derby china, hosted my parents' catered dinner parties. Even from my perch overlooking the banister two floors above I could hear and smell the glamorous gatherings: cigarette smoke and smoked salmon; roast duck and Cabernet; pinging glasses and laughter; cigar smoke, coffee, and the hot chocolate slathered over the profiteroles. Sometimes a friend of my parents would come to my room to chat with me. Jimmy and I were not invited to the parties, even to say hello. Sometimes I snuck down to the kitchen using the elevator to bypass the parties and nibbled on the leftover hors d'oeuvres. The next morning I tasted the rest of the party dinner—frequently for breakfast before I left for school.

Guests to our home entered into the first-floor foyer. It was formally and opulently decorated with a woolen green carpet, and on one wall a painted mural of a dark forest with large green leaves, purple and blue flowers, and a peacock, as spooky as the scene it portrayed. (The peacock was painted out after the downturn of my father's business. He was superstitious and believed birds brought bad luck.)

The guests could ride to the second floor in our tiny elevator, but most chose the staircase opposite the mural with its dark wood banisters sitting atop white poles with knobbed newel posts on the end. The foyer was spacious enough that it held a grand piano and, during the Christmas season, my brother's elaborate model train table as well.

Between the living room and the dining room was a long hall that accommodated two extra chairs and a credenza that served as a bar.

My lookout station onto the world was the living room bay window. It was framed by long, muted-yellow silk drapes that fanned onto the gray carpeting. As a pre-teen I sat on the wide windowsill for hours looking for Sid Caesar—the star then of the TV show *Your Show of Shows*—who would gaze down at the sidewalk as he slouched along the street toward what I was told was his psychiatrist's office. Or I waited for Lillian Hellman to emerge from her brick town house directly across from our house, even though I didn't really know who she was. And I always hoped to see the naughty, pregnant girls emerge from their Catholic home for unwed mothers. *Why*, I wondered, *did they always emerge from their refuge in groups? If they were bad enough to have to leave their homes in Ohio or Kansas or somewhere and see their pregnancies through in New York, hidden from the people they knew, why would they want to call so much attention to themselves by walking around in groups of six or seven? One pregnant girl is nearly invisible. A gaggle of pregnant girls waddling down the street causes stares.*

A large portrait of my mother wearing a black-lace long-sleeve evening gown, her curly, reddish-blond hair cascading onto her shoulders, hung over the yellow couch.

The portrait, by David Immerman, had hung in the corner window of Saks Fifth Avenue as an example of his work to help raise money for war bonds. The artist had offered to paint the portrait of the person who bought the most bonds. According to the October 1, 1945, issue of the *New York Sun*, a vice president of Saks Fifth Avenue announced that the winning war-bond purchase was $750,000.

The living room housed our Christmas tree. Many German-Jewish families in my parents' social circle celebrated Christmas because they wanted to identify with other Americans. Around three o'clock on Christmas morning, while the household was asleep, I snuck downstairs and unwrapped all my presents and then re-wrapped them so no one would know. The gifts from Saks Fifth Avenue were my favorites because the paper was shiny and the Scotch tape peeled off and reattached easily, so I got away undetected. Presents with ribbons were a challenge because the bows had to be refolded in exactly the same places. Some gifts had no covers but just sat near the tree, like my life-size doll I named after my best friend Babsy. No one had a clue about my Christmas Eve escapades. My mother was astonished when I confessed to her many years later.

My parents' room on the third floor was decorated with light-lavender, purple-trimmed silk brocade draperies fanning out on the floor like my mother's silk wedding dress in the photo on her marble-topped French bureau nearby. Their twin beds next to each other were covered in heavy pink brocade bedspreads. The two marble-topped French side tables were made of inlaid wood and matched my mother's dresser. In front of the drapes was a chaise longue that no one ever rested on.

My father kept a pistol in the top drawer of his side table; the bullets were in his bureau. I knew this because sometimes in my early teenage years whenever my parents went out and I was in the mood, I snooped through the drawers, discovering my father's gun and my mother's book of dirty limericks. (All the drawers could be locked, but my parents left the keys in the locks.) My father was given a permit for his gun because he sometimes carried the payroll for his business from the bank to his offices in the West 20s.

His gun scared me. Guns belonged in Westerns on television, not in our home. Years later when I was in my late thirties he temporarily left my mother to live with a woman in Miami. He arrived at this woman's home with his suitcases. When she wouldn't let him move in, he threatened her with his gun. Fortunately, shortly after the incident his behavior appalled him. He returned to my mother in New York, where she was staying for two weeks, and was hospitalized for a few days afterwards. I assumed he had a mini nervous breakdown.

Down the hall on the third floor was the den, with bamboo fabric walls, a green rug, a burnt-orange couch, and an old-English leather-with-gold-inlay-covered desk. The bathroom off the den, which was directly under Miss Hanna's room, housed my father's woodworking table. The television was in the den, and when my parents went out Miss Hanna and I watched it together. It was my parents' space, in which Miss Hanna didn't belong. If they came home early, she would get up and leave.

Jimmy's room faced the front of the house on the fourth floor. Like most young boys, he had a desk, bed, chair, and dresser, but his wallpaper befitted an elderly Englishman. It was maroon toile with a repeated hunting scene of dogs, horses, and foxes. Prints of hunting dogs hung on top of the paper. Jimmy adored my father's brother Irwin, who had a similar room in his home.

Miss Hanna's room, which was next to mine at the back of the fourth floor, had once been a bathroom. There was just enough space for a twin bed and a dresser along one wall. Her closet was flat against the other wall; it wasn't deep enough for a clothes rod. There were only hooks that could each hold a few hangers. Two of the walls were exposed red brick; the wall closest to her twin bed had wallpaper in the same pink and white lace toile pattern as in my room. From both our rooms we had the view of an old, skinny tree and a red-brick convent, St. Catherine's Convent of the Sisters of Mercy, later torn down to make way for a red-brick public elementary school, PS6.

At the front of Miss Hanna's tiny room, forming the fourth wall, was a set of French doors that led into my bedroom, three times the size of hers. She had to walk through my room to reach the bathroom and the rest of the world. She spent too much time on tiptoe.

Miss Hanna's room was as cold as it was tiny—freezing

even in the fall and spring. She kept her doors closed so she wouldn't make my room chilly too. One evening at the dinner table I overcame my fear of getting Miss Hanna fired and told my mother that Miss Hanna's room was cold.

"Queenie upstairs is complaining that she's cold," my mother said to my father, using her favorite nickname for Miss Hanna.

In the end, Miss Hanna did get a portable heater, but she had to turn it off when she went to sleep so it wouldn't start a fire.


Miss Hanna was physically so near that I had only to moan if I didn't feel well in the middle of the night. They were deep, staccato moans that came from wanting her attention as much as from pain. Immediately Miss Hanna was next to me, down on the floor on her knees so that her face could be close to mine and she could stroke my hair.

"What's wrong?" she would ask me.

"My stomach hurts," I probably said. My stomach often hurt. I threw up all the time.

When I was in bed and when I slept, I sucked my thumb. In the formal photographs of me as a child, I have beautiful front teeth because the space made by my sucking my thumb was retouched out. When I was four, my mother became very unhappy with my growing buck teeth. To get me to stop sucking my thumb my mother first found a bad-tasting nail polish developed for the very purpose of halting thumb-sucking. It stung my tongue and tasted the way furniture polish smelled.

When that didn't work, my mother and Miss Hanna tied my hands to the bedposts with gauze strips. I didn't fight them during the process, but it terrified me. Not only couldn't I put my thumb in my mouth, but I also couldn't move. I hope I screamed my head off in protest when Miss Hanna tried it again the next night. I promised Miss Hanna that I wouldn't suck my thumb any more if she didn't tie me to the bed again. I kept that promise.

Mother was not pleased with my nose. Once a week when I was five, she came upstairs at bedtime to say good night and to try to make my nose shorter. "Ibbidy bibbidy ibbidy bibbidy ibbidy bibbidy sab," she recited and pushed the tip of my nose up at each word. I lay back on my pillow and took the nose-pushing passively. At first I thought it was a game. When I tried to push back onto her nose, she pulled away. (She had had her nose fixed, I learned years later. She probably didn't want me to hurt it.) I thought her game was silly and strange and I just lay there and looked up at her while she pushed.

After Miss Hanna tucked the sheets around me in bed, she kneeled on the floor, and together we recited the Lord's Prayer, which she had taught me. I sometimes accompanied Miss Hanna to St. Ignatius Loyola, the Catholic church around the corner from our house. She attended services on Sunday mornings. I watched her cross herself with holy water, kneel before she walked us to a pew, and walk up to the altar to take communion. Sweet incense filled the air and sermons echoed off the vaulted ceilings and stained-glass windows. I couldn't compare the church with a synagogue because I had never been to one.

I was upset when I saw Miss Hanna in her regular clothes,

which she wore on her days off—often a maroon suit or a dress from her cold closet. She was her own self then instead of my personal nanny. I didn't want to share her with anyone. Nevertheless I sat on her bed and watched her put on rouge that was too red for her face. In those days rouge was creamy and came in a circular tub. She tried to spread it out evenly as my mother did, but her rouge ended up in splotches, as rosy as Howdy Doody's cheeks. But at least the color distracted from her dark eyes, which sometimes looked as sad as a basset hound's.

Miss Hanna was going to Port Jervis, she said on her days off, or to visit her friend Victoria. I didn't like being left alone with my mother when a part of me felt missing. Mother dragged me to Saks or Best & Company to try on clothes, or to visit her mother in an apartment on 96th and Park that smelled of rotting fruit, body powder, and cigarette smoke. I accompanied Mother to the Breck salon on 57th Street near Fifth Avenue and watched while she had hair treatments, an alcohol-smelling liquid massaged into her scalp. Occasionally I got a scalp treatment, too. We visited her sister Ruth-Elaine and my cousins, Andy and Allen, who lived on East 90th

Street near Gracie Mansion. On a few weekends Miss Hanna took me with her to visit her friend Victoria. My best visit was the weekend we went to the Danbury fair. I won a glass sugar bowl by tossing a nickel into it. A few days later it slipped from the shelf where I had put it and fell onto one of Mother's good dinner plates. It broke the dinner plate but emerged from the collision unscathed. A triumph of poor over rich, I decided.

I can clearly see Miss Hanna sitting on the gray chair next to a window in my room with a thimble on her finger darning my father's socks. She put a wooden darning egg into each sock, then wove the threads in and out as she made a patch to cover the hole. I played solitaire or Labyrinth on my bed and looked up at her as she sewed. She looked sad, as she always did when her face was at rest. Her deep-set black eyes stayed sad even when she smiled. I assumed she was sad because when she was a little girl like me she lived in an orphanage and didn't have any parents. From my earliest years I knew she had been an orphan. Always I imagined her orphanage looking like the red-brick convent outside our windows.

When she sewed, Miss Hanna's stitches were perfectly spaced and tiny as in the finest antique quilts. I sat next to her on the chair as she taught me her sewing skills. She bought me a child's sized thimble and showed me how to cut a small length of thread, put the end in my mouth to make it straight and pointy, and thread the needle. She showed me how to take a tiny stitch into one piece of fabric and then the other and pull the needle and thread through. I repeated the process until the fabric pieces were sewn together. She showed me how to knot the end so that the tiny, perfectly spaced stitches would stay put. I learned to sew quite well, but never got the hang of the thimble. Miss Hanna had to use a thimble because the ends of her fingers had dry calluses that cracked easily. Sometimes before bed she covered her hands with Vaseline and white cotton gloves and slept that way.

Miss Hanna made an entire wardrobe for my favorite doll including a black-velvet coat and hat finished with real white rabbit fur trimming. For my bed she crocheted an ivory cotton-thread bedspread in a multi-star, early-American pattern. The bedspread, which I have today, has a five-inch-long fringe on three sides. Sitting on the floor and repositioning herself as she needed to, she tied on hundreds of strands one at a time by hand. She then spent more hours on the floor carefully combing the fringe to get out the tangles—the way she combed my long, dark hair before putting it into two braids that hung down my back.

# 5

We loved musicals, Miss Hanna and I. Passionately. Luckily, we lived during the Golden Age of the Broadway musical and together we saw *Brigadoon, South Pacific, Finian's Rainbow, Call Me Madam, The King and I,* and many more. Sometimes my friends had their birthday parties at shows and we all attended together. But mostly I went alone with Miss Hanna. My parents generously bought all the tickets I wanted. The shows meant more to me than anyone knew, even Miss Hanna. They were the happiest times of my childhood. I listened to the albums incessantly.

The moment I heard the first three notes of the *South Pacific* overture—da-de-daaah, Ba-li-Ha'i—the music took over inside of me. And it still does. The orchestra repeats the three notes six times—first punctuated by the timpani, then the brass, incessantly louder and faster until on the seventh repeat the glorious melody bursts forth—"Bali Ha'i may call you, any night any day." The music drew me onto an island in the South Pacific in the early 1940s. I'm told that the reason the notes are so haunting is that the third note is chromatic; it doesn't belong in the scale, and so it is jarring. It tells us something is wrong. What was wrong was World War II.

The music in the musicals opened me to feelings that I hadn't seen or felt in the real world: get-out-there-and-dance happiness, longing, romance, and love. I wanted to live in those shows. Not just be an actress, I wanted to be the characters, be their friends, breathe the air in their fictitious towns.

When Tommy left his life in New York City forever for the once-in-a-hundred-years village of Brigadoon, I wanted to be the Fiona he returned to. I wanted to help

Jeannie pack on the evening of her wedding, to be a bridesmaid in the "Come to Me, Bend to Me" ballet.

I longed to run away from my life to a palm tree-covered island in the South Pacific where it was always summer and romance would surely follow. I wanted to hand Nellie a post-shampoo towel, and most of all I wanted to be Liat and lie in Lt. Cable's arms as he sang "Younger Than Springtime" to me. I was only nine when I first saw *South Pacific*, but I had my first sexual stirrings watching Lt. Cable and Liat make love. The musicals were an escape, a fantasy that I could almost make real by singing the songs to the cast recordings.

During the afternoons after school when I was in my pre-teen years, when Mother was out playing cards or Mah-Jongg, Father was at his office, Joe was preparing dinner, and Miss Hanna was upstairs reading or sewing on the chair in my room, I was in the living room on the second floor singing show tunes at the top of my off-key voice. From my stage in the back corner of the living room behind an upholstered yellow chair and next to the Capehart record player, I performed for the long, yellow drapes. I moved my arms as the characters had in the shows, and walked back and forth pretending I was an actress. I knew all the words, as one might expect after listening to the same songs dozens of times. I still know them—including the entire "Soliloquy" from *Carousel*—as do my childhood friends.

Singing show tunes in my little corner carried me away from home and school into a world of happy endings. I did well at my ballet lessons, so I thought that maybe I could someday be on the stage. And amazingly all of that singing to records eventually taught me to carry a tune.

# 6

I could be the best-behaved child on the planet, and I could keep everything Miss Hanna said and did a secret from my parents, but with each passing year what I did or thought was less and less a factor in preventing her from being fired. A black, brick wall loomed closer and closer. I would grow up and not need a nanny any more. I didn't think about what I would do without her. It was too frightening. Instead I worried about what she would do without me. Where would she live? Who would keep her company? She had no family and only one friend, Victoria.

But I did grow up and became aware of a deep, gnawing conflict: Gradually the glamour of my mother's world was seducing me with its makeup and pretty dresses. I was allowed to go shopping by myself and picked out the same gray princess-line jumper and pink-checked blouse that all my friends had. I talked to Miss Hanna about boys, but I came to respect her answers less and less. She wasn't married, nor had she ever had a boyfriend that I knew about. I was convinced Miss Hanna was a virgin. Yet I was responsible for Miss Hanna. She was mine, after all. I felt guilty about leaving her when I went to parties. I remained loyal to her, but she was becoming inconvenient.

When I was thirteen I agonized over taking a Christmas trip to Florida with my grandmother. I didn't want to leave Miss Hanna. At my mother's suggestion, I wrote down a list of the pros and cons of going to Florida. Leaving Miss Hanna was the biggest con. The allure of swimming and sunshine finally won, and I decided to separate from her for those two weeks. After I told her I was going, she explained to me that she hadn't been feeling well and would spend a week in the hospital having tests.

She must have hidden her aches and pains from me for a long time. Or I was too self-occupied to notice. "Miss Hanna and I" had always been all about me.

I returned home from Florida to the news that Miss Hanna had cancer. Hodgkin's disease. I didn't fully comprehend what that meant. My life continued as it was, filled with school; with parties; and with ballroom dancing at the Viola Wolff classes for well-to-do, mostly German-Jewish teenagers in a turn of the century town house. We were the children and grandchildren of and pretenders to the "Our Crowd" set, some of whom deemed themselves superior because they arrived in this country before the Jews of Eastern Europe and Russia.

Increasingly, Miss Hanna stayed in the cold little room next to mine, turned on her portable heater, and read a book alone. She did exercises to try to keep her legs strong. Because she couldn't afford real leg weights, she filled a cloth bag with dried peas. She attached the weight to her leg at the ankle, sat on a little wooden table in her room, and lifted each leg from the knee. My father gave her shots of vitamin B12 to make her stronger; he got the vials of the vitamin from our family doctor, who was also Miss Hanna's doctor and a family friend. My father knew how to give shots because he gave himself shots of Demerol when he got migraines, several episodes a year.

During this time Miss Hanna wanted to make herself useful to justify living with us. I can't imagine that my parents paid her very well or even at all after she got sick. They probably paid her medical bills. To their credit they didn't mention firing her—at least not in my presence. They kept her for my sake and also for theirs: I was happy with her, doing well at school; their hands were full enough with Jimmy and his poor grades and psychological problems so bad he saw a child psychiatrist.

Miss Hanna sewed for my mother and crocheted to earn extra money. She made eyeglass and change purses out of gold-covered thread and lined them with shiny, golden fabric; she sold them through The Women's Exchange on Madison Avenue near 63rd Street and to my parents' friends. When fashions changed and skirts got longer, she couldn't afford new clothes—so she crocheted hems onto her old skirts to add to their length.

To cross the street in New York in the 1950s, before public spaces were handicapped-accessible as they are today, you had to step down off one curb and, once you got to the other side, step up on another. Some curbs were built higher than others. Miss Hanna began to alter her route to the store, going out of her way to cross at corners where the curbs were lower. I grew annoyed listening to her talk about curbs all the time. She began using a cane.

One spring day when I had just turned fifteen, Miss Hanna and I went out for a short walk together—down the steps of the stoop, down the sidewalk to Madison Avenue, across the street past the window of the Burlington Bookshop, and under the maroon awning of Campbell's funeral home. Then we turned to re-cross Madison Avenue and head back home. At the curb on the northeast corner of Madison Avenue at 81st Street, where the new red-brick school had replaced the red-brick convent, she fell down onto her knees. I tried to help her up by holding onto her arm, but she couldn't get up. I got behind her, put both my arms under her shoulders from the back and tugged upward. She couldn't have weighed more than ninety pounds by then, but either I wasn't strong enough or I was too scared to raise her off the street. A stranger, a man passing by, lifted her up. Her stockings that already had runs in them tore further and her knees were scraped and bleeding, as mine had often been when I was a child and she was there to pick me up. As we limped toward home, I felt both terrified and abandoned—as abandoned as a person can feel when her loved one is alive and walking next to her.

Even after the fall, I denied what was happening to her, although deep down I suspect I knew. Perhaps I was also denying what was going on within myself. A boy I was dating asked me how I could stand having her live in the room next to mine. That thought had never crossed my mind. She was where she belonged, where I wanted her—close to me even though I was psychologically moving away.

Early one evening the next autumn I was in the fourth-floor hallway bathroom when I heard Miss Hanna call downstairs to my mother: "Mrs. Salz, I'm sick." I froze from the inside out. I was terrified that Miss Hanna was sick and hated that she was reduced to asking help from a woman who reviled her. I imagined my mother's annoyance, her pursed lips, a few snide remarks to my father and even more to her friends.

Miss Hanna went into the hospital the next morning, and she never came back. She spent a few months in a rehabilitation facility; then, too sick to return to my parents' home and without money of her own, she wound up in a public nursing home for cancer patients called The Towers on 106th Street and Central Park West. The red-brick building (previously the New York Cancer Hospital, which moved to the East Side and became Memorial Sloan Kettering) opened as a nursing home in 1956, the year Miss Hanna entered. It gained notoriety during the nursing home scandals of the early 1970s and was closed down in 1974. Miss Hanna told me that the patients got clean blankets only when the public health officials came by for an inspection.

Every Saturday morning, for most of my junior year in high school, I took the bus across the park and transferred onto the Central Park West bus to go uptown and visit Miss Hanna. The Towers stank of dirt, disinfectant, and sickness. Miss Hanna's bed was one of maybe twenty placed helter-skelter and crowded into a round room in one of the turrets. Her bed was by a window—with a view of another institutional red-brick wing. She had a small, round, white basin under her bed that she used when she threw up. She was bone-thin and frightened.

Early in the spring of my junior year, Miss Hanna told me that all she wanted was to see *South Pacific* once again. It was having a revival at the City Center of Music and Drama. I used my allowance savings to buy tickets for us, but when the time came, I didn't take her. I was afraid that she would fall down again and I once more wouldn't be able to help her—or that she would die in front of me. Jimmy took Miss Hanna to see *South Pacific* without me. Until that time I hadn't known that Jimmy even cared about Miss Hanna. Eventually seeing her became more pain than I could bear. I wanted to run away.

That opportunity came when my junior year was over and we left for our annual summer visit to the Jersey shore. I think, I hope, I went to say good-bye to Miss Hanna. In mid-July, while I was busy chasing boys at the beach club, especially lifeguards and "older" boys in their early twenties, Miss Hanna's friend, Victoria, arranged for her to move to St. Rose's Home, a Catholic hospice for cancer patients just south of the Brooklyn Bridge, where she wrote me that the Sisters took very good care of her. We exchanged letters frequently. I have only one now. It says,

*Dear Nancy, I received your lovely letters. They mean so much to me. I love to get them… I feel fine. Can not wait to see you. I was glad to see Jim. Please tell Joe I was asking for him. Give my love to your mom and dad. With all my love, Miss Hanna*

But I never went to visit her. I told myself I would see her in the fall when we were back in New York. Once back in the City, I let my mother talk me out of visiting. Too terrified to face Miss Hanna alone, I ran away into my own life. I was seventeen, applying to college, and I had been hiding my feelings for Miss Hanna from others most of my life. Now I hid them from myself.

I desperately wish I had had the courage to hold her in my arms, to stroke her hair, to tell her that I loved her, that she had been a wonderful mother to me—to tell her that her life lived on in me. I was old enough to do for her what she had done for me. But I didn't. So in the end, I abandoned her.

The call came on my phone one evening in early October of 1957 while I was sitting on the gray chair in my room doing my homework. Miss Hanna had died. I ran down the hall to tell Jimmy. We cried together a little, but not deep sobs. Not yet. Mother was home that night and she heard me tell Jimmy. She came upstairs to talk with me. She pushed aside my school books and sat down on the small end table next to my chair.

"This is the end of one phase of your life," she said.

I thought her words were unfeeling and superficial, that she was glad Miss Hanna was dead. But in her own way, she was trying to comfort me.

My first feeling was relief. I wouldn't have to take care of Miss Hanna or feel guilty any more. I could grow up.

Jimmy, Victoria, our cook Joe, and I were the only people at Miss Hanna's funeral, held at the Walter B. Cooke Funeral Home on Third Avenue at 87th Street. My parents didn't attend, and I didn't expect them to. The room with its stained-glass chapel and maroon carpet had space for about fifty people. Only Victoria accompanied Miss Hanna to her burial in a huge cemetery in Queens where the headstones stood side by side as far as the eye could see. I went back to my teenage life of school, applying to colleges, Broadway shows, and parties. I denied how important Miss Hanna was to me, and I denied my grief—until I went into therapy for a time a few years after college.

"Tell me about your family," the psychiatrist began on my first visit to him.

"I have a brother, a father—and I had a governess," I said, finally breaking down into the sobs that I had been holding back for years.

Sometime in my late twenties, I stopped thinking about Miss Hanna so often. If her name came up when my childhood friends talked about their nannies, I said nothing. Their mothers had respected their nannies. They didn't know about my childhood, and I wasn't going to tell them. My vow of silence was now an automatic response to any discussion of nannies.

Elizabeth Cecilia Hanna.

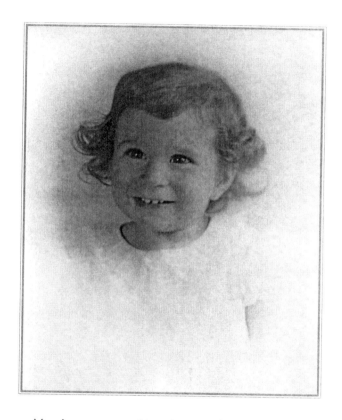

Me, about one year old, with a space between my teeth
from sucking my thumb.

My mother, Jimmy, my father, and me, about three
and clearly smitten with my father.

My mother as a teenage Powers model.

My mother. Stunning and innocent.

My father and mother happy early in their marriage.

Miss Hanna after she stopped wearing a uniform.
The garden in New Jersey.

Miss Hanna, me, and Jimmy.
The only photo I have of Miss Hanna and me together.

A photo of me taken by the roving Central Park photographer.

The house on the right was ours.

Jimmy and Miss Hanna at the entrance to the Bronx Zoo.

Ignatz Salz ("Iggy"), my Grandfather
who was shot by gunmen.

Theodor in a suit, Birdie in a hat, Mother, Ruth-Elaine, and Oscar,
probably outside a summer cottage in Margaretville, New York,
about 80 miles from Middletown, where Miss Hanna was born.

Jenny (my grandmother's mother), Irwin, Jacque, James, and Laura
at Marienbad in the late 1920s.

The Towers Nursing Home building, now part of a condominium.

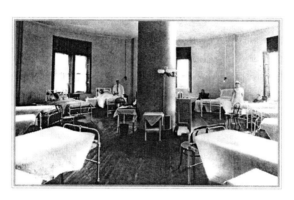

(Photo courtesy of Memorial Sloan Kettering Cancer Center. Used by permission.)

A room in the Towers Nursing Home when it was the New York Cancer Hospital. Imagine this room with twice as many beds.

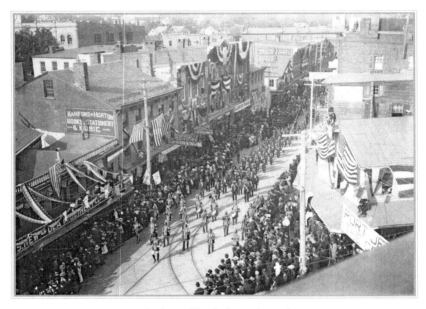

A parade down North Street around 1900.
From Marvin H. Cohen's *Middletown*.
(Arcadia Publishing. 2001. Used by permission.)

St. Mary's Orphan Asylum, where Miss Hanna grew up.

A page from the 1900 Middletown Census.
The arrow in the far left column points to the Hanna family.

**Children Discharged from November 1st, 1909, to November 1st, 1910.**

| Age. | Name. | When discharged. | To Whom. |
|---|---|---|---|
| 7. | Parker, Milton | Jan. 26, 1910 | Mrs. Parker | Port Jervis |
| 3. | Parker, Dorothy | Jan. 26, 1910 | Mrs. Parker | Port Jervis |
| 13. | Hanna, Elizabeth | Mar. 22, 1910 | Miss Ryan | Spuyten Duyvil |
| 11. | Kirby, Mary | Mar. 23, 1910 | Mrs. Casey | Maybrook |
| 11. | Titsworth, Martin | May 23, 1910 | Mrs. Downey | Pine Island |
| 11. | Smith, Myrtle | April 10, 1910 | Mr. Smith | Uniontown, Pa. |
| 12. | Smith, Mildred | April 10, 1910 | Mr. Smith | Uniontown, Pa. |
| 7. | Smith, Louis | April 10, 1910 | Mr. Smith | Uniontown, Pa. |
| 12. | Stefinskie, Vincent | May 27, 1910 | Mrs. Rigney | Monticello |
| 12. | Kirby, Nellie | June 6, 1910 | Mrs. Sweeney | Monticello |
| 12. | Litts, Elizabeth | June 13, 1910 | R. C. Protectory. | |
| 13. | Sheldon, Eveline | June 13, 1910 | R. C. Protectory. | |
| 11. | O'Mahoney, Roderick | Aug. 1, 1910 | Miss Maguire | Port Jervis |
| 4. | Franze, Loretta | Sept. 1, 1910 | Mrs. Franze | Slate Hill |
| 11. | Finnen, Edward | Sept. 6, 1910 | Mr. Reiley | Vails Gate |
| 8. | Kane, Mary | Oct. 1, 1910 | Mrs. Heart | Wintertown |
| 7. | Kane, Margaret | Oct. 1, 1910 | Mrs. Heart | Wintertown |
| 5. | Kane, Mabel | Oct. 1, 1910 | Mrs. Heart | Wintertown |
| 3. | Kane, Myrtle | Oct. 1, 1910 | Mrs. Heart | Wintertown |
| 13. | Brown, Clara | Oct. 31, 1910 | Sisters of Charity | Newburgh |

WALTER H. BREWSTER,
Superintendent of Poor.

Miss Hanna's discharge record from the orphanage.
Prepared by the "Superintendent of Poor."

# 7

For the next decades Miss Hanna lay dormant inside me, deep where I had hidden her. I never recognized that the loving woman I was becoming grew mostly from her lessons. Gratitude never entered my mind.

When I was fifty-nine, my vow was still rock-solid. I remember one incident from that year because a change began to take place in Mother's and my relationship. We were at the Ocean Beach Club in Elberon, New Jersey, where my parents had been long-time members. Mother was staying there for the summer.

By then my brother and father were both dead. Jimmy

died when he was fifty-five from stomach cancer probably related to his alcoholism. My parents came up from Florida and had a small funeral for the family—at Campbell's, of course. They left New York before a crowded and loving memorial service was given for Jimmy by his friends and admirers at Alcoholics Anonymous.

My father had a heart attack while resting in his room at the beach club when he was eighty-six. I was fifty-seven, and spending the summer in Lenox, Massachusetts. A tornado watch prevented me from driving to be with my mother the day my father was stricken. He died a few days later after my mother authorized taking him off life support. She made the decision herself but consulted me before implementing it.

"I'll call the hospital," she said. "Then I'll call Campbell's to come and get him."

"Aren't you forgetting a step?" I asked her.

"What?" she asked.

"He has to die first," I said. "Campbell's won't come unless he's dead."

To her credit, she laughed. We laughed together— just the two of us. It signaled that our mother-daughter relationship was about to get a new start.

In the intervening years, Mother and I had rarely talked about anything substantial. My parents had moved to Palm Beach, Florida, when I was in my late twenties and came north to New Jersey in the summer to visit with their friends. I saw them twice a year for a day or two each visit. But some momentous events had happened in their lives.

About twenty years earlier, when I was thirty-six, my father left my mother for another woman—the woman he had been keeping secretly in Miami and at whom he had pointed his gun. Only a few days passed before he came crawling back. I wanted my mother to kick him out permanently, but she wanted him in her life. To Mother, life was a prom, and she never wanted to be without a date. My father's leaving prompted me to try to close the distance I had put between my mother and myself since I was four. I invited her to take a trip with me, and she accepted right away. The following May we sailed for Paris on the QE2 and spent three days there shopping and eating.

My mother knew her way around first class on an ocean liner. She found us a table and people with whom to share our meals: a besotted young couple—he married to another woman, she a lover along for the crossing—and a father and son from Minneapolis traveling together. Much to my delight, the father, a sweet-looking chubby man of about sixty with a gentle smile, developed a crush on my mother. She introduced him to caviar, and he wrote her a love letter which she showed to me and which I found saved among her belongings after she died:

> *Dear Betty: At a very real risk of being too personal, may I say the pleasure of your company and your unusual attractiveness has been a highlight for us—and me. Though we may not meet again, please accept what was difficult for me to say.*

That was just what she needed. I was thrilled for her. I also hoped she had learned the difference between a real gentleman and my father.

Once in Paris, she got us reservations for delicious dinners at outstanding restaurants I wouldn't have had a clue how to find. These included Le Grand Véfour, at the time a three-star Michelin restaurant. At our dinner at Chez Allard on the left bank she leaned over to a table of three French couples and asked in English if she could take the watercress garnish they had left on their serving plate. I was mortified, but they adored her. She laughed and glowed as the men flirted with her. I watched this *femme très charmant* with admiration.

After our trip, when Mother and I were closer, I still didn't break my vow. It wasn't difficult keeping the vow. By now it was automatic. Additionally, speaking about Miss Hanna would only have enraged her and pushed her away. *Are you still thinking about that ugly woman?* I imagined her saying. And I would feel the nearly unbearable pain and shame once again. Better to leave my love for Miss Hanna protected inside me. Mother probably came to believe that Miss Hanna didn't matter to me anymore. That was okay with me.

During those years I spoke to my mother on the phone, I in New York, she in Palm Beach, only once a week for half an hour on Saturday mornings. I'd get onto the top of my bed and wait for the phone to ring, which it did promptly at 10:00 a.m. I loved being her daughter for that short time. We talked about the world she assumed was as important to me as it was to her, and I played my role: hair styles, clothing, parties, shows I had seen, gossip about her friends and their daughters. I never told her about boyfriends because it took only a few words like "Jerry? What happened to John?" to bring back the feelings similar to those when she criticized Miss Hanna. Eventually she stopped asking. She showed little interest in my career as an advertising copywriter and later as an account person. She didn't feel comfortable in my world. Repeated requests to visit my office and become acquainted with my work friends were met with refusals.

When I was forty-three I left the advertising agency world and began my consultancy, preparing and presenting training seminars to young marketers on how to work with their advertising agencies. After years of my bosses' indifference, I had finally realized that while I might not be smarter than they, I wasn't dumber either. Once I decided I was going to work for myself, I had a devil of a time figuring out what to do. I yearned to be admired and validated, and to make more money than I was making, which wouldn't be too hard given my pathetic salary. What I didn't know was how much Miss Hanna would influence my final choice of business.

I read many career guidance books and completed all their tests. It seemed my aptitude lay in a giving profession—helping people. The giving that I had learned from Miss Hanna as a child, beginning on the boardwalk in Asbury Park, was blossoming inside me and giving me great satisfaction. I would teach, I decided, something to do with my current profession, advertising. When a friend in marketing complained that she couldn't figure out how to work with "the strange people on her agency team," a light bulb went off. I would teach young marketers how to do that. After interviewing dozens of people, I wrote a book, and when the book was published, I became the person who wrote "the book." Soon thereafter I quit my job as a vice president in a small agency. I loved teaching, seeing my students grasp a concept. I was very successful, even in my first year. As far as I know, I was the first person who ever trained marketers to work with their advertising agencies.

Mother loved to brag to her friends whenever I got an important new client—always a top advertiser and Fortune 500 company. Sometimes I wondered if she was just using me to brag to her friends. Other times I felt that she was genuinely proud of me.

Mother must have watched the clock when we were on the phone because she cut off our conversation promptly after a half hour—long distance costs were on her mind, I assumed. I didn't even tell her about my partner, Richard Mickey, until we had moved in together in Lenox, Massachusetts, adding a second location in addition to my apartment in New York City to call our home.

I spoke to my mother on the phone far more frequently than I had ever spoken to my father when he was alive. With him I didn't speak, I listened. Nothing ever changed in that regard. They had moved to Palm Beach, where he carried on with his philandering, eventually with my mother's blessing. He also bragged about his girlfriends within their social circle. The only reason their friends didn't shun my father was because they adored my mother, and she wanted to keep him. Two years before he died, he went on Prozac and became a much gentler man. He even took my mother on a cruise. It was too late to earn my trust. I eventually stopped being angry at him but my fear stopped any love in its tracks. I accepted him for who he was and moved on with my life. When we spoke, I couldn't wait to get off the phone. And when he died, I saw the black cloud over my head disappear. I tried but could cry for him only once when I thought about what might have been.

"Your father is dead, and my stomach ache is gone," Mother said to me a few weeks after he died.


The summer day I visited Mother, I was fifty-nine and my father had been dead two years. The sky was filled with thin white clouds for my six-hour visit to my mother at the beach club in New Jersey. As always I joined her friends at a big table on the screened-in porch overlooking the pool, with rocky jetties and the rolling dark gray ocean in the background. In the afternoon, we pulled two white Adirondack chairs together under a canopy closer to the ocean and talked about nothing memorable. Perhaps where she was going for dinner.

Perhaps which bridge game she would play in the next day. By now her hair was short, mostly gray and dark brown. She had stopped bleaching it years before. But she was still pretty and fashionable in white pants and an oversized pastel blouse. She called to her friends' grandchildren who were playing around the pool to come over to her and say hello. Some did. I felt sad that neither my brother nor I had given her any grandchildren of her own.

Around four o'clock Mother walked me to my car and said, "I love you." She paused then added with astonishment more to herself than to me, "I really do."

This time I started to believe her. She had said the words "I love you" on occasion my entire life, but I dismissed her comment as easily as I dismissed "Your call is very important to us" when recited by a robot voice on the phone. I had never let it in, and I didn't that day at the beach club either. *Jimmy and Father are dead,* I thought cynically. *Now it must be my turn, the only choice she has.* But another part of me softened ever so slightly.

Richard, a deeply loving man, a cellist with a handsome face and a brilliant mind, visited Mother with me in Palm Beach every January for her birthday. We had dinner with her friends and spent time with my favorite uncle, Sam (the husband of my mother's deceased sister Ruth-Elaine), and his second wife, Arlene.

Before our visit in 2003, when I was nearly sixty-three, my mother's best friend Liz called me in New York.

"I want to prepare you for seeing your mother," Liz said. "Betty has deteriorated. She is very depressed. She wore a stained, old housecoat when we came over to play bridge. And no makeup. You know how your mother was always so fastidious."

I hadn't noticed any depression when we spoke on the phone every Saturday morning. But when Richard and I arrived I saw that Mother was indeed very depressed. She didn't want to get out of bed. I stood over her, forced her to make an appointment with her doctor and took her there myself. The mother-daughter role reversal had arrived, and it was time to step up and take responsibility for her. I would have preferred to run away, but this time I did not. I was not going to do that ever again. It was my job to be her caretaker—bossy, as accused by Mother—and do it well.

We sat in the doctor's waiting room together. I had seen many other daughters accompany their mothers to the doctor. Now it was my turn. Surprisingly, the doctor didn't give her any medication, but he told us both that she was depressed. Even with her doctor's diagnosis, my mother refused to accept that her feelings were depression. As we walked out of his office she thanked me for making her see the doctor, actually respecting me. I felt very proud of myself. She invited me to have coffee with her at her local drugstore. I couldn't recall that ever happening before. I felt like we were friends.

The following month her dear friend Liz died suddenly, and Mother became more seriously depressed. She had a few appointments with a psychiatrist, the husband of a woman who owned a handbag store on Worth Avenue, which made my mother both comfortable and impressed. He gave her a prescription for antidepressants, but she never gave them a chance to work. She didn't understand what was happening to her emotionally. One day she called me with a revelation ...

"I know what's wrong with me," she announced. "I'm having mood swings."

It was painful to watch her decline. Her lack of self-awareness was astonishing and made it more difficult for me to care for her.

"Stop treating me like a child," she said emphatically when I made a suggestion that I thought would make her life easier. (I suspect every daughter of an aging mother has heard those words.)

I went to visit her that June (2003) because she didn't feel well enough to visit New Jersey. Richard didn't accompany me on this visit. When she opened her apartment door to greet me, I felt her love for me—perhaps for the first time. For that moment, I let go of my defenses and fear. I was happy. I melted into her love. She went back to bed —she spent most of her days in bed watching television now or looking out her window at the ocean—and as I walked to the nearby hotel where I was staying I thought, *This is what I've always wanted.*

That afternoon while she was sitting in bed, she

allowed me to brush her hair. Then she said to me.

"I can't believe I'm having these feelings." I knew she meant loving me.

We hugged while I cried a lifetime of tears—allowing her to see how much her love meant to me.

"Why didn't you have them sooner?" I asked.

"I had a difficult time back then," was her only explanation.

I didn't push for more details. But I wondered if she meant that she had known about my father's affairs. Or maybe it was about being at my father's beck and call. I felt her love deeply and was satisfied with her explanation: finally, for the first time, I had confirmation that she hadn't been able to love me, that she had abandoned me emotionally to Miss Hanna. That realization meant as much to me as her love. It confirmed that I had not been imagining anything in my past; it was a validation of my life-long perceptions.

Later that day I was looking at a photo she had on her wall of me in a bathing suit with makeup covering my birthmark. Finding even more courage I asked her,

"What did you think of my birthmark?"

"It upset you so much," she said.

"I know, but what did you think?" I pushed.

"You were so upset." She said.

"But what did *you* think?" I pushed harder. Finally she said:

"It didn't come from my side of the family."

Once again I had my answer. I felt vindicated, not hurt. I also felt liberated and more than a touch superior to her. This was confirmation of her limitations and wasn't about my birthmark or me. We really didn't live in the same world.

Asking any questions about Miss Hanna—why she hired her instead of a different woman, why she kept her so long, why she disrespected her, why she was so jealous, why she disliked her so intensely—never crossed my mind, even when we were being more open with each other. That discussion would have spoiled our new relationship. And I was still protecting my love for Miss Hanna.

Leaving Palm Beach engendered mixed feelings: *Let me out of here and back to the life I've built* versus *I want to stay in her love*. As the plane back to New York headed out of West Palm

Beach toward the turquoise ocean, I pushed my face near the window to watch for Mother's apartment building, trying to hold on to her as long as I could. But being with her was bad for me, even with the newfound love. We were worlds apart. I had grown, and I didn't want to go back. Yet I had to tear myself away and return to my own life.

That October, I visited her again in Palm Beach. I was looking forward to another warm, loving weekend. But when I called her from the hotel to say I had arrived, she made a mean, ridiculing comment to me. I wish I could remember what she said. I only remember the hurt I felt and the tears that poured out of me.

There I was in a gorgeous, luxury hotel room surrounded by pastel pinks and corals and blues and greens. Sweet-smelling soaps in the shape of seashells sat on the marble bathroom sink. The calming blue ocean was just beyond the sliding glass doors and the balcony. But I might as well have been in my childhood spindle bed looking at the convent's red-brick wall.

*No one knows how to hurt me the way she does,* I thought. *And when she's dead, no one will be able to hurt me as much again. I can get through this.* My self-pity was soon replaced with stoicism.

Mother was mean for the next two days, her gift for cutting ridicule not tempered one iota by her depression. She insisted I drive all over town, giving me wrong directions so that she would miss her doctor's appointment, arriving after his office hours were over. On the last night of my stay, after a pleasant dinner at the home of her good friend Paula, I found some courage and asked her why she was being so horrible to me.

"You have to understand how hard it is for me for you to see me like this," she said.

By now she had to use a wheelchair to go to and from her apartment. She wore a nightgown all the time so that she wouldn't have an accident before she could get out of her clothes on the way to the bathroom. I didn't understand, that evening. I was too wrapped up in the hurt she was causing by pushing me away. But by the next morning I did understand how she was feeling, and once again found my resolve.

"You can push me away as hard as you like," I told her. "But I'm going to keep on loving you no matter what you do."

I wasn't ever again going to let her change me from the loving woman I had become back to the hurt, angry child. This moment was one of the proudest of my life and was filled with love—love that was born from Miss Hanna, the woman for whom my mother had zero respect.

In early January 2004, an aide taking care of Mother called an ambulance to take her to the hospital. Richard and I found out the next morning and arrived at the hospital that evening. She died six days later, two days before her eighty-eighth birthday, from intestinal organ failure. She was in bad pain off and on for a couple of days—I had to leave the room when she screamed—but the hospital and eventually the hospice finally made her comfortable. I worked hard to enforce her written living will and her written DNR instructions. (You have to fight to have this happen in a hospital even with everything in writing.) One day in her hospital room Mother groaned loudly in my direction, and somehow I knew she wanted to make sure I was following her instructions. I told her that I was, and she calmed down. She wanted to die. Mother only opened her eyes once; they were filled with terror. She never spoke, although she nodded her head the first time Richard and I saw her in the hospital.

We had two memorial services: one in Palm Beach and one in New York. Over a hundred people attended in total—mostly her remaining friends, a few of their children and children of deceased mothers who had been my mother's friends, my friends, and what was left of our family. I ordered flower arrangements featuring green-tinted roses to frame a photo of her—looking as beautiful as an older woman as she had when she was younger. At the New York service, held at Campbell's around the corner from our old home, Richard played his cello at the beginning of the ceremony. At my request, he also played Saint-Saëns' "The Swan" during the ceremony. Mother's ashes are entombed with my father's at a cemetery in Westchester County.


The following Thanksgiving, Richard and I returned to Palm Beach to tie up the remaining legal details about her will and to visit my Uncle Sam and step-Aunt Arlene. I adored them both. Mother spent time with them but never forgave either for finding each other just six weeks after my mother's sister, Sam's wife Ruth-Elaine, had died.

Sam was the only relative I had left of my parents' generation. We went to his golf club for the celebration, and I sat next to one of my mother's oldest friends, Norma. I asked her to tell me about my mother, and she talked about the years when my brother and I were children. I remember her saying something and then adding,

"And she had to put up with the awful Miss Hanna."

My blood ran as cold as it did the night Miss Hanna got sick and called down the stairs to my mother. But this time I paused. I had not broken my vow since Miss Hanna had died but I thought, *It's time. Time to let the world know how much I love Miss Hanna. Do it now.*

"Miss Hanna was wonderful," I said.

"Then why did your mother hate her so much?" Norma asked.

"She was jealous." That's what I told Norma, although I knew it was much more. She might have hated Miss Hanna because she felt guilty about never picking up Jimmy when he was a baby. She might have felt guilty about not being much of a mother to me—or as good a loving mother as Miss Hanna was. I didn't know it, but that moment was my first step toward finding Miss Hanna. A step that would lead to my search for her a few years later.

# 8

Once I had felt Miss Hanna inside me again, I could not get enough of her. I was bringing her back to life memory by memory, feeling by feeling. My search for her became urgent and consuming. Although I was still working at my consulting business, preparing and conducting training sessions, the major recession that began in 2008 lowered the frequency of my seminars. I was glad. I relished the free time to continue my search for Miss Hanna.

At the New York Office of Vital Records, I had filled out a form to obtain Miss Hanna's death certificate. They wrote back and denied me a copy because I wasn't a relative.

It was only a minor setback. I now had the definite date of Miss Hanna's death and the first success of my search. It was all very exciting, private and personal—new and old at the same time—the past coming into the present, the present into the past. Like putting old movies of my childhood onto a DVD. Miss Hanna was consciously living inside me—not just an as extension of me but this time as a person in her own right.

The next stop on my search was the Internet. I went first to Ancestry.com. It's a terrific resource. Type in a name, type in a date, and see what comes up. Sadly, no matter how many variations of Elizabeth Hanna's name I inputted, the output was the same: nothing.

I didn't want to telephone St. Rose's Home, the cancer hospice where Miss Hanna had died. The home—run by the Dominican Sisters of Hawthorne, which was founded by Rose Hawthorne Lathrop, the second daughter of Nathaniel and Sophia Hawthorne—had a policy of not accepting donations from the friends or family of former patients. I was sure they wouldn't tell me anything. But they were my last resort. I picked up the phone and called them.

A friendly, older-sounding man named Edwin answered. He took down what little information I had, Miss Hanna's name and the date of her death, and tried to locate her in their records right then and there. This was a good sign. After keeping me on hold for close to ten minutes while I played Spider Solitaire on my computer, he returned to the phone and reported that he couldn't find her. He promised to keep trying, but given their policies I doubted he would.

I felt I had hit a wall. I didn't know where I would search next. Then much to my surprise Edwin called me back the next day. I was on a business call—furious that I had to let my voice mail pick up. Once I was finished with my call, I left the desk in my home office and ran to the answering machine that for space reasons was in my bedroom. I hit the playback button.

"Nancy, it's Edwin," his message said. "I found her!"

I dashed back to my desk, so excited that my hands shook as I looked for the number of St. Rose's Home. Of course, I hit the wrong numbers as I dialed so I had to redial. And redial again. Finally—

"Edwin, it's Nancy. You found her! You're wonderful!

Tell me everything."

"Elizabeth Hanna was born on December 24th, 1895, in Middletown, New York," he said. "Her father's name was Elias Hanna and her mother's name was Raffa DuMont."

This was a huge step forward. I had found her parents, and I was elated. You'd think I would stay that way. But as the hours and then days wore on, that elation not only faded, it turned to anger. What kind of mischief were my feelings up to now? Finally it dawned on me that I was jealous—how could she be *their* daughter when she was *my* governess, *my* nanny? I still did not want to share her even with her own, dead parents. I was five again. My sense of humor snapped me out of my childish feelings of jealousy.

Then I remembered Miss Hanna had grown up in an orphanage. It didn't jibe. If she had parents, why was she an orphan? Maybe I was wrong about her past.

A few days later I remembered that Miss Hanna had worked for another family that I knew. I Googled the name of a man whom she had also taken care of as a child. Within thirty seconds I found him, his address and his phone number. I decided it would be prudent to write to him first and enclose my e-mail address, rather than call him out of the blue. That was a good decision because he didn't have a clue who I was. When we finally spoke, he told me that he didn't remember very much about Miss Hanna, although he had kept a throw blanket she had crocheted for him. And he confirmed that she had been an orphan. It felt validating to speak with someone who shared my past, who shared Miss Hanna. But he asked me not to contact him again. For reasons he wouldn't disclose, he didn't want to talk about her. He died two years later.

I confidently returned to the Internet and logged onto the visitors' site for Middletown, New York, to search for an orphanage. There wasn't one there. Perusing the pages, I noticed a mention of the nearby city called Port Jervis. Port Jervis? That rang a bell. Miss Hanna visited Port Jervis on her days off. Each tiny snippet of information brought me closer to Miss Hanna and her to me. It fueled my excitement.

I searched Google again, this time for orphanages and Catholic orphanages in Port Jervis. And there it was: St. Mary's Orphan Asylum.

That had to the one where Miss Hanna was raised. I

was getting Miss Hanna back one tiny jigsaw puzzle piece at a time.

I called St. Mary's right away. They no longer had records, but referred me to the Sisters of Charity, who had run the orphanage. The Sisters of Charity had no records either but referred me to the Catholic Guardian Society. My feelings of discouragement were tempered by the kindness of everyone I spoke to. No one asked me if I was Catholic. No one felt bothered or thought it strange that I was searching for someone who wasn't a member of my immediate family. In fact the people I spoke to seemed to identify with my search. But they all came up with nothing. There weren't any records of Miss Hanna's time at St. Mary's Orphan Asylum. I was told, however, that St. Mary's, and many other orphanages as well, kept very poor records. Often the records that were kept were intentionally destroyed.

Although I could not prove Miss Hanna grew up at St. Mary's, I was convinced that she did. It was the only orphanage where all the facts—her birthplace, her parents, her trips on her days off—came together.

Now I was filled with more questions: Why did she

grow up there if she had parents? What was her childhood like before the orphanage? I needed to know more.

## 9

Middletown, New York, Miss Hanna's birthplace, was a newly incorporated city of about 12,000 when Elias Hanna emigrated there in 1889. The place was thriving. Factories had begun to spring up after the arrival of the New York & Erie Rail Road in 1843, and the city kept growing. Shoes, lawnmower blades, furniture, beer, files, condensed milk, and hats were all made in Middletown. The twenty-one-year-old Elias could have stepped off the train and walked into a factory with a waiting job.

According to the national census, Elias Hanna emigrated from Turkey. (The local Middletown census reports that he was from "Arabia." However, many census-takers reported all immigrants from the Middle East as Arabian.) While there are no specific records about Elias Hanna's life in and before Middletown, if we assume that he was a typical immigrant from the Turkish Ottoman Empire, we can get a good picture of him and how he spent his days.

According to Frank Ahmed's unique social history, *Turks in America: The Ottoman Turks' Immigrant Experience*, between 45,000 and 65,000 Anatolian Turks immigrated to the United States before World War I. They were Christians, Sephardic Jews, and Muslims.

Elias Hanna's hometown was on the Anatolian plateau, near the Taurus mountains, in what is today the country of Turkey. He was a farmer with a long mustache and a strong work ethic. He may have been a bachelor; if he did have a wife and family, he would have planned to find work in the United States for good wages and then return home in a year or two. When he decided to immigrate to America, he found his way to a port on the Black Sea, sailed to Europe and then took another ship to America. His only goal was to make money. To save his wages he lived in a crowded rooming house with other male Turks who put their mattresses on the floor, many to a room.

While he quickly got a good factory job in Middletown, he was not greeted with open arms by the city's residents. More likely, he was met with a great deal of prejudice. Like much of America, Middletown was not tolerant of its immigrants in the 1890s. The *Middletown Press* headlined an article about the Immigration Act of 1892 with the words "To Keep Out the Scum." In nearby Port Jervis a black man was lynched by a mob in June of the same year.

Turks kept to their own people. They visited their own coffeehouses. They had to learn very little English to get along.

On occasion, a Turkish immigrant man would meet a woman and fall in love. According to Ahmed, their wives were frequently Americans of European heritage. Perhaps Elias Hanna had no family in Turkey and this is how Elias Hanna met Raffa DuMont, Miss Hanna's mother. But there is no record of their marriage. In fact, there is no record of Raffa DuMont at all that I could find. The 1900 Middletown

Census shows that Elias was married to a woman named Mary and had two children at home, Elizabeth (Miss Hanna) and Phillip. I had forgotten that Miss Hanna had a brother. But there is no record of that marriage either; Elias and Mary might have lied to the census. Perhaps Elias left Raffa for Mary. I vaguely—but very vaguely—remember Miss Hanna telling me that she was a bastard. That was her word, if my memory is correct.

Before she was put in the orphanage at the age of five, Miss Hanna's home could have been a haven in a hostile world. Her father's English would have been halting, but he could have loved Miss Hanna's mother. After all, he gave up his hope of returning to Anatolia, perhaps for her and his children.

It is possible that Miss Hanna grew up in a loving household—until her mother died when she was five. Now a widower, Elias put his daughter and son in an orphanage where they remained until they were approaching fifteen and deemed old enough to leave and live on their own.

# 10

To understand orphanages, it's best to put aside everything you already know: Little Orphan Annie, Oliver Twist, "Please sir I want some more," a vision of serious, wide-eyed children lying on wrought-iron beds, fifty to a room. In reality, that vision is only partly true. There was nothing romantic about American orphanages. Life in an asylum could be hard and cruel.

In the decades before the turn of the last century, children didn't actually have to be orphans to be raised as orphans. They could have both parents living or just one. There was even such an institution known as a half-orphan asylum—the Chicago Nursery and Half-Orphan Asylum opened in 1859. The main criterion for being in an orphanage was that a child be poor, needy, and unlucky. Far too many children qualified, including Miss Hanna.

Between 1860 and 1890, the number of orphanages in this country more than tripled, from about 170 in 1860 to 564 in 1890. By 1910 that number had risen to 972, and about half the children in the orphan asylums had one or more parents still living but unable to care for their children themselves.

The overwhelming attitude toward the poor in nineteenth-century America was "blame the victim." If you were poor, you were immoral and your situation was your own damn fault. Poor equaled scum. Not only were orphans like Miss Hanna hungry and dirty, they were filled with shame because of their situation.

Few people took into account the effect of several overwhelming changes in our society: thousands moved into cities for low-paying jobs; millions immigrated to the United States from Europe; and diseases were rampant in the urban slums. The cholera epidemics of 1832-3 and 1849 caused many deaths and left many children without one or both parents. Most people didn't see any relationship between a child appearing to be neglected and the poverty in which his or her family was living.

Throughout the century, however, there were a forceful few who devoted their lives to trying to help poor families. Unfortunately, these reformers' views were dissimilar and confused: Send the poor to the poorhouse. Grab children off the street and put them on trains, orphan trains they were called, to live with families in the Plains states. The trains stopped along their route, and childless couples would peruse the children, selecting some and rejecting the rest, who then hoped to be chosen at the next train stop. Eventually, children were taken away from their poor, dirty families and brought up in alternative homes called orphanages.

Altruism was not the only motivator of the reformers. Charles Loring Brace founded the New York Children's Aid Society in 1853. He shipped children on the orphan trains to the Midwest to live with families. But the only children who qualified were white and Protestant. Brace called the poor "the dangerous classes." The New York Society for the Prevention of Cruelty to Children was founded by Elbridge Gerry in 1874, but volunteers for the various local SPCCs actually roamed the streets looking for children to rescue and took them away, whether their families wanted it or not.

Many of the orphan asylums were run by religious groups. Protestants, Catholics, and Jews all had their own— as did, eventually, local and state governments throughout the country. Most of these orphanages were more like prisons than homes: harsh, cold, frightening places where bullying prevailed and there was no hope of leaving even for a few days until the children reached their mid-teens and could leave for good.

But other orphanages, especially later in the century, though very strict and regimented, were run by people who believed in letting the children visit their parents or a parent, if there was one, and go to school with non-orphaned children. Eventually these people even came to believe in the importance of play in a child's life and saw to it that the children had access to yards or playgrounds.

St. Mary's Orphan Asylum was one such orphanage.

It was founded in 1875 at 56 Ball Street in Port Jervis, New York, a charming city on the Delaware River, in the corner where New York, New Jersey, and Pennsylvania touch near the Pocono Mountains. St. Mary's Church stands today and the remnants of the orphanage form the rectory for the church. Depending on the year, it was home to 150 to 200 orphaned boys and girls.

On one of the first warm days of spring in 2008, still feeling that I was venturing into forbidden territory but excited to walk the streets Miss Hanna had walked, I drove out from New York City for a visit. I'd put two and two together by that day and realized that my outdated fear of ridicule had caused the shivers on the first day of my search. I was breaking the vow I made as a child never to speak of Miss Hanna. Slowly I let my guard down and opened myself up to the memory of my mother's ridicule. Unfortunately, I couldn't have the warm memories of Miss Hanna without the cold memories of my mother's attitude. I decided I could deal with this and headed onto the Interstate to western Orange County, New

York, over the state line from the farthest northwest part of New Jersey.

As I turned onto Ball Street in Port Jervis, my eyes were drawn to the tall steeples of the large red-brick church at the far end of the street. This is where Miss Hanna went to church. The largest steeple was set off by azure sky and the slope of a distant hill. St. Mary's was the tallest building in sight. The houses on Ball Street were small and badly in need of fresh paint. They must have looked better when Miss Hanna walked by them—maybe on a school outing, perhaps in uniform with black braids bouncing on her back. But the church itself had been restored and looked just as it did when it was built in 1851.

My many visits to Catholic churches with Miss Hanna allowed me to feel comfortable, even at home, in St. Mary's. I walked toward the altar to light a candle for Miss Hanna and visited the the rectory, a small part of the original orphanage that hadn't been torn down, to try to feel what it was like when Miss Hanna was an orphan there. During my visit, I met one of the church deacons, a spunky woman whose mother had worked at St. Mary's and spent a lot of time with the orphans.

Much to my surprise the deacon reported that St. Mary's Orphan Asylum was a "very happy place." The hallways, though narrow, weren't a cold, institutional brick like the outside of the building—or like the room next to mine where Miss Hanna had lived. They were painted tan. The sun brightened the orphanage through many windows.

But how happy could an orphan be, missing one or both parents? Seeing a parent perhaps on a visiting day only to have that parent abandon the child again and again to the sisters—nuns who may have been caring, even loving, but still weren't parents? "Happy" had to have been a relative term at any orphanage. I suspect true joy was unknown.

Miss Hanna's days most likely started at dawn with prayers in the chapel followed by breakfast and school at St. Mary's school next to the church. Her afternoons would be consumed by chores—mending, cleaning, and supervising the younger children in the school or the playground—and learning a trade like cooking or sewing. (So this is where Miss Hanna learned her tiny, perfect stitches!) She would attend another prayer service followed by dinner and bed.

Orphans in asylums were brought up in the attitudes of the day. Girls were trained to be good and obedient wives or servants. Boys were trained for jobs in a manual trade. No wonder Miss Hanna was so accepting of her life as a nanny, of her place in society.

Soon after my visit to St. Mary's, I learned via the 1910 Census that Elias Hanna, her father, had been living in a boarding house nearby. He listed himself as a widower. Only then did I remember that Miss Hanna told me that her mother had died when she was very young. Miss Hanna must have entered St. Mary's shortly thereafter, and surely before 1910. At that time I thought it was the only reason for her sad eyes.


The census information about her father was the last of the facts I could find about Miss Hanna. The search had come to a dead end, and I reluctantly put it aside. I had also begun to write a story about Miss Hanna, but I put that aside too and moved on with my life—continued with my consulting, began to write articles for a small newspaper. I had learned enough to satisfy my curiosity. I had reconnected with Miss Hanna in the real world and the Miss Hanna inside myself— or so I thought.

## 11

Nearly twelve months after my visit to St. Mary's, months in which I rarely thought about Miss Hanna and my story, I returned home to a voice mail from the assistant at St. Mary's Church. With restrained excitement she told me she had received a list of former orphans, compiled as a typing exercise by the young granddaughter of a volunteer genealogist for the local historical society. "Elizabeth Hanna" was on the list. I had been right all along! All of the excitement of the search welled back up. Miss Hanna was once again a conscious presence inside me.

The typed records indicated that Miss Hanna entered

St. Mary's on November 14, 1900, when she was almost five; her younger brother, Phillip, probably entered at the same time. Miss Hanna stayed at St. Mary's as a ward of the state until March 22, 1910, before her fifteenth birthday. She was released in the care of a woman named Miss Rose in the Spuyten Duyvil section of the Bronx, where she undoubtedly became a nanny for the first time.

I also learned from the church assistant that the source of the newly typed records was an efficient and generous woman named Nancy Conod. I called to thank her, to tell her how much her and her granddaughter's work had meant to me.

She must have been inspired to learn more about Miss Hanna because a few days later she e-mailed a short article from the Friday, August 12, 1910, *Port Jervis Union*:

*Mrs. Helen Rodgers was shot dead in the yard of her home, No. 66 Cottage St, Middletown, Tuesday afternoon by Elias Hanna, a peddler, who sent a bullet into his own brain and fell dead near her body. The only witness of the crime was the little daughter of the murdered woman. Hanna had been a boarder in the Rodgers home, but recently was forced to find board elsewhere, because of his unwelcome attentions to Mrs. Rodgers. Tuesday afternoon he begged Mrs. Rodgers to take him again as a boarder. When she told him he would have to ask her husband, he shot her.*

I was stunned, a bit a nauseous, and so frightened for Miss Hanna. Had her father been violent when she was a child? Did he ever hurt her? I remembered the fear I felt when I saw my father's gun in the table beside his bed. But he never killed anyone.

I began to wonder if Miss Hanna knew about her father. Did the Sisters tell her even though she was no longer at St. Mary's? The murder and suicide happened a few months after she left the orphanage.

Miss Hanna never said a word to me about her father's past in all the years she took care of me. Surely she must have known that he was a murderer. Now we both had fathers who carried guns, who used them to threaten or kill, who were unstable men. I knew how frightening that was. I knew a little about how she felt. And now I understood another reason for her sad, sad eyes.

What I didn't understand was how Miss Hanna could love. From the orphanage, to her tiny cold room next to mine, to the Towers, and finally to St. Rose's, she was surrounded by institutional red brick. Perhaps because of the Sisters who raised her, her religious faith, and the very few years she had with both her parents, she was filled with love. And she gave all the love that she had to me.

I believe that she identified with my estrangement from my parents. She wanted to make sure that I knew I was loved, that I didn't feel as lonely as she had felt when she was a child. It took the search for Miss Hanna to fully appreciate how beautiful the woman my mother called "ugly" made me feel.

# 12

I planned a visit to St. Rose's Home, but it had closed in 2009, just one year after I had spoken to Edwin and learned about Miss Hanna's parents and birthplace. Had I waited to call, I might never have discovered Miss Hanna's past.

Inside I had always been ashamed of abandoning Miss Hanna in St. Rose's Home—shame, not guilt. I had made a cruel mistake. It had happened. It was over. I felt bad and moved on. But I cried for days after writing about not visiting Miss Hanna in the cancer hospice. I cried for her sadness and hurt. I cried the deepest as I understood more deeply what my love and attention would have meant to her.

How much better I might have made her feel.

Writing this memoir helped me recognize the depth of the gifts Miss Hanna gave to me. I discovered the person behind the love and how truly remarkable she was. In my childhood Miss Hanna was an extension of me. For many years she lived only in my feelings. Finally I could release her to be the brave and loving person she was, independent of me. I am in awe.

Miss Hanna had nothing, really. No family she could point to with pride. No husband. No children except those she was paid to raise and whom she raised as her own. She had only one good friend, which, it turned out, was enough. She had her religion, which she rarely discussed but which was her foundation, I believe. And she had her heart.

Now that Miss Hanna has once again come alive inside me and alive in her own right, I know this to be true: When I am my most loving, I am Miss Hanna.

# Partial Bibliography

Frank Ahmed, *Turks in America: The Ottoman Turks' Immigrant Experience*, Columbia International, 1993.

LeRoy Ashby, *Endangered Children: Dependency, Neglect, and Abuse in American History*, Twayne Publishers, 1997.

Marvin H. Cohen, *Images of America—Middletown*, Arcadia Publishing, 2001.

Timothy A. Hacsi, *Second Home: Orphan Asylums and Poor Families in America*, Harvard University Press, Cambridge, MA, 1997.

Dale Keiger, "The Rise and Demise of the American Orphanage," *Johns Hopkins Magazine*, April 1996.

Justin A. McCarthy, *The Turk In America: The Creation of an Enduring Prejudice*, The University of Utah Press, 2010.

# Acknowledgments

If only I could thank my lifelong friend, Wendy Weil, an incomparable literary agent, in person. She was first to encourage me to write this story, but she died suddenly in the fall of 2012. Wendy, I miss you every day.

My heartfelt thanks ...

To my cyber friend Julie Lane Gay, who read and re-read drafts and provided countless important suggestions, cheerful, encouraging e-mails and endless caring. To my readers, Richard Mickey, Claudia Shuster, Kathy Roeder, Dori Katz, and all my insightful classmates in my Stanford Online Writing Studio courses and the Lenox Workshop, for their honest feedback.

To my Stanford teachers, Malena Watrous and James Arthur, who taught me about narrative, the importance of detail, and omitting what need not be written.

To Nancy Conod, who found the newspaper article about Miss Hanna's father and all the historical information about St. Mary's Orphan Asylum. She helped complete the story and did so with great, good cheer.

To the friendly and thorough research staff at the Thrall Library in Middletown, New York, who contributed articles about attitudes in Middletown in the 1890s, and did so over the Internet free of charge.

To Amy Lafave of the Lenox Library Association, who helped me navigate the complicated world of census data.

To Marvin H. Cohen, author of the wonderful photo history *Middletown*, who granted me permission to use a photograph from his book.

To Matt Tannenbaum of The Bookstore in Lenox, Massachusetts, who generously provided design advice.

To my helpful editor, Susan Dalsimer.

To my imaginative and talented cover and book designer, Susan Newman.

To Nancy Harris Rouemy, who first said my story should be a book. Her enthusiasm first motivated me and then carried me through all my drafts.

To my dear partner, Richard Mickey, who has lived by my side through the many years of research and drafts with patience, encouragement, and copious amounts of love. How did I get so lucky!

(Photo: Ormond Gigli)

Nancy Salz is the author of many profiles and musical theater reviews
for Berkshire County newspapers and online arts magazines.
This is her first narrative book. She lives in New York and Massachusetts.
www.nancysalz.com

CPSIA information can be obtained
at www.ICGtesting.com
Printed in the USA
FFOW03n1828020614
5658FF